PETER G. BIETENHOLZ

HISTORY AND BIOGRAPHY
IN THE WORK
OF
ERASMUS
OF ROTTERDAM

GENÈVE
LIBRAIRIE DROZ
11, RUE MASSOT

———

1966

1re édition: novembre 1966

" — O glaub's, heig d'Mensche gern!
'S isch 's einzig Glück! — "

(Jacob Burckhardt : *Vorgsicht*)

GERTRUDIS BING

MEMORIAE

SACRUM

ACKNOWLEDGMENTS

The author wishes to thank all those who supported his efforts and laboured to neutralize his deficiencies in the English language. A few must be mentioned by name, Professor Samuel Kinser of Northern Illinois University read the entire manuscript and gave the sort of encouragement only a friend can give. Truly generous was the help of Dr. Hans Baron since it was tendered in spite of basic disagreement with some principal theses of this study. Professor Werner Kaegi of the University of Basel and four of the author's colleagues at the University of Saskatchewan, Professors Peter Marsh, Ivo Lambi, Terry Heath, and Joe Fry, read and constructively criticized parts of the following text. The author's wife, Doris, endured it all with her usual good grace.

CONTENTS

INTRODUCTION

The historical works composed by Renaissance humanists are impressive both in number and in originality of approach, but they still await a comprehensive survey. Fortunately Erasmus was not himself a historian; so we need not consider the bulk of humanistic historiography in this study. Two aspects only of the humanistic contribution to historical thought and writing should briefly be outlined here, since Erasmus was instrumental in the development of both. Humanistic scholarship impregnated the methods and techniques of historical writing, and Erasmus' role in this process has been generally recognized. Less attention has perhaps been paid to the growing concern for the meaning of history. It is here that Erasmus' part was rarely matched by his contemporaries and remained largely unnoticed by modern scholarship.

The impact of humanism on the techniques of historical writing may be outlined in this way. From the time of Petrarch the encyclopedic works of medieval compilers were being repudiated in favour of the complete works of individual authors, preferably the classics. As manuscripts were brought to light, reproduced, and collected in proper libraries, historical sources multiplied and the picture of the past was integrated. From the prominent place of classical historians in Petrarch's list of favourite books to the 16th century editions of a first corpus of early Church historians or Byzantine chroniclers, the preserving efforts of humanists served Clio in manifold enterprises.

Once gathered together, the classics of history could be compared with each other. The appreciation of distinct subject matters, treated by the classical authors with appropriate technique and style, led to the ambition to imitate, to equal, and to surpass them. Sallust's and Thucydides' studies of distinctive conflicts, Livy's account of the growth of a unique city, Plutarch's achievement of comparative biography, all provided the humanist historians with some of their characteristic subjects. In other instances the imitation of one peculiar model gave way to an eclectic method which examined and embodied the merits of various approaches. Initiated in the 15th century [1], the ideal of a perfect historical method based on eclecticism was fully developed by Bodin.

---

[1] Cf. F. Gilbert, *Machiavelli and Guicciardini: Politics and History in Sixteenth-Century Florence*, Princeton 1965, 204f.

The progress from preserving to restoring efforts marked the birth of modern philology. Again it was Petrarch who paved the way. He devoted himself to the reconstruction of the mutilated text of Livy. He was convinced that the experience of the ancients enlightened the living; it was, therefore, important to know exactly what they had said. [2] Valla showed in his critical study of the *Donation of Constantine* how the style and expression of a text provided criteria for the date and the circumstances of its composition. After Valla's death his text-critical approach was to have the impact of a fanfare whose echo resounded from many quarters. Erasmus, in particular, was bound to influence the countless numbers who read him. In his *New Testament* and in the preface and notes accompanying his patristic editions he demonstrated how the adequate interpretation of a text depended upon comprehending characters and concepts from the peculiar historical setting which had produced them. Clio thus became the hand-maid of literary criticism, but in serving she profited immensely. Cultural epochs were set off against one another on stylistic and literary grounds. Political and religious institutions were seen to be subject to historical change. Works and letters in reliable and complete editions became the basis for intellectual biography.

Nevertheless, the humanistic contribution to historical writing was not one of blueprints so much as of workers. The methods of humanism changed the face of historiography because of the large number of historians recruited from the humanistic camp. Outside the sphere of Renaissance humanism there had been only a few officially appointed chroniclers. Now realms and cities had their histories rewritten by trained humanists. Independent scholars combined professional skill with the patriotic or pious devotion of medieval amateurs. They amassed sources and scanned them critically. They discarded legends, but invented fictitious speeches that voiced their own historical meditations. Having studied eloquence and moral philosophy, they drew upon their skills to enlighten the present with the examples of the past.

Humanistic assiduity produced not only new histories; it produced new views of history. In the minds of early Italian humanists the meaning of history came to envelop new complexities which derived from the renewed study of the ancient authors. Subsequently, at the turn of the 16th century, humanism developed a routine approach to history. In the generation of Erasmus there is some indication that this routine was being challenged, though the challenge would not reach its peak before the 17th or even the 18th century. At first the reaction against the humanistic understanding of history was never more than partial and in some cases—notably so in the case of Erasmus—it was born from the very principles of humanism.

It may be doubted whether at any time there existed a homogeneous humanistic concept of history, but some general characteristics emerged fairly regularly. History became increasingly secular and individualistic as the

---

2 Cf. M.P. Gilmore, *Humanists and Jurists*, Cambridge Mass. 1963, 16 and passim; consequently it only took one more step to criticize the ancient authors for what they had said: see L. Valla's *Duo Tarquinii, Lucius ac Aruns, Prisci Tarquinii filii an nepotes fuerint: adversus Livium ... disputatio* (*Opera omnia,* ed. E. Garin, Turin 1962, 1. 438 ff.)

humanists attempted to recreate the man-centered cosmos of classical antiquity. Conversely, new patterns and recurring types were developed, for history was still expected to teach the present and the future.

Not all that was new in Renaissance historiography must be associated with humanism; the humanistic trend, however, was conspicuous in the imitation of Cicero. His regard for the political and moral functions of history in maintaining the state on sound principles was reflected in the republicanism of Petrarch and Bruni. Cicero's demand for a subtle balance between historical truth and rhetorical message was pondered by Valla and Pontano. It led to the general problem of the relationship between poetry and history and to the question of whether the latter was to relate personal experiences or rather to describe the events of a remote past. The resulting deliberations of the Italian humanists were enlivened by the growing awareness of the Greek philosophical approach to history as presented in the works of Aristotle, Herodotus, Thucydides, and Polybius. The Greek theory that historical situations recurred in regular cycles buttressed the humanistic concept of a glorious renaissance after a dark intermediate age. It also supported Cicero's contention that the lessons of the past provided the models for moral and political conduct.

Patriotism was further stirred by the visible relics of the past. The ruins of Rome inspired Biondo's antiquarian research. In his wake, other humanistic historians north and south of the Alps based their studies on the documentary sources and surviving institutions of specific regions.

With the 16th century, religious fervour and dissension came to overshadow singleminded patriotic devotion. Historical theory, on the other hand, while it had been tackled prior to the Reformation, was now perfected as an alternative to active historiography. Patrizi, Bodin, Baudouin, the prominent humanists engaged in historical methodology, were all men of divided loyalties. Once again the lead of classical antiquity proved fertile : in addition to ancient rhetoric and philosophy, Lucian's treatise on the writing of history provided widespread inspiration. Yet, contrary to the ancients, the humanistic treatises on historical method were more concerned with those who read histories than with those who wrote them. The fact that the reader too was considered in need of advice attests not only to the swelling volume of historical literature but also to the growing complexity of historical thought.

In a sense, historical methodology was thus an alternative to humanistic historiography; but in other ways it was an extension. The theoreticians too were convinced of the exceptional merits of history, and their treatises continued the praise of history seasoned with Ciceronian eloquence which can be traced back to the early days of humanism. Yet the first half of the 16th century also focused a new and highly critical look at the achievements and the enthusiasm of the humanist disciples of Clio. Melanchthon's historical work does not tie in with Sabellico's isolated undertaking of a universal history written in the humanistic taste. Melanchthon resumed the great spiritual tradition of the medieval chronicle. He explained how God had directed the world since Adam and Eve. Together with the medieval theological outlook he quite logically resumed the medieval systems of periodization. Although he knew and often used the humanistic techniques, he became the representative of a new sort of confessional historian whose objectives and achievements lay beyond the program of humanism. Erasmus too was critical of many aspects of the humanistic approach to history. He may have resembled the confessionnal historians in that his criticisms had ultimately religious motives. Beyond that, he expressed a profound concern with the truth of all historical knowledge acquired by man, a concern that advanced the humanistic spirit of inquiry and forecast many facets of the complex historical thought of the modern age.

ERASMUS AND HISTORY

I

"Non peccat qui credit historiae. Sed quid fructus?" Erasmus asks this question in his *Commentary on Psalm 33,* published in 1531. His words referring to one particular incident of the Old Testament must indeed be taken to express his general attitude towards history.[1] For, as he goes on to say, some read the Bible with the same profane approach as they read Herodotus and Livy. "The letter kills and the spirit brings to life." Erasmus does not think that the letter necessarily kills, but there is no profit in expounding the literal sense. Such efforts will not lead to life, unless one attains Christ, the *logos* behind the letter. A little farther on in that same text Erasmus returns to the profane historians: Livy, Thucydides, Herodotus, Plutarch, and the lot of them, they are just men. They make mistakes, deliberately or unconsciously. Among several contradictory versions often none is true. The sad conclusion is *"rerum et verborum varietas"*; the historical fact and the historical account are at variance with each other.[2]

---

[1] All scholars seem agreed that Erasmus was not a historian, but that his method of text criticism exercised considerable influence upon contemporary historians: M.P. Gilmore, Fides et Eruditio: Erasmus and the Study of History, *Humanists and Jurists,* 87-114; W.K. Ferguson, *The Renaissance in Historical Thought,* Cambridge Mass. 1948, 40f.; P. Joachimsen, *Geschichtsauffassung und Geschichtschreibung in Deutschland unter dem Einfluss des Humanismus,* Leipzig 1910, 105ff.; G. Kisch, *Erasmus und die Jurisprudenz seiner Zeit,* Basel 1960, 67f.; S.A. Nulli, *Erasmo e il Rinascimento,* [Turin] 1955, 235ff.; A. Renaudet, *Erasme et l'Italie,* Geneva 1954, 181f.; R. Pfeiffer, *Humanitas Erasmiana,* Studien der Bibl. Warburg 22, Leipzig 1931; E.H. Harbison, *The Christian Scholar in the Age of the Reformation,* New York 1956, 92.

[2] *Des. Erasmi Roterodami opera omnia,* ed. J. Leclerc, Leyden 1703ff., 5.369ff. (hereafter: LB ...): "...Legimus a Mose serpentem aeneum erectum in deserto. Historia est, fateor, et quidem verissima. Sed nihil aliud est quam historia? Credi poterat, nisi Dominus ipse figuram aperuisset in Evangelio dicens: *sicut exaltatus fuit serpens in deserto, ita exaltari oportet filium hominis* (371DE). (After other examples of figurative interpretation): Haec eo pluribus inculcare visum est, quo simul et illorum errori mederemur, qui non multo religiosius legunt sacras historias quam Herodotum aut Titum Livium, et eorum fidem ac vigilantiam excitarem, quibus persuasum est in omnibus Scripturis divino spiritu proditis latere Christum. *Littera occidit,* inquit Paulus, *spiritus vivificat.* Non semper occidit littera, sed est ubi occidat prorsus, est ubi nihil aut minimum prosit, sed non vivificat, nisi perveneris ad Christum. ... Qui legit serpentem aeneum sublatum in stipitem et a serpentium morsu liberatos qui in illum intenderant oculos, non peccat si credit historiae. Sed quid fructus? Si credit hoc naturae vi factum, nihil est fructus. Si virtute Dei, aliquid est fructus, sed non liberatur a pecca-

The opening passage of Erasmus' *Commentary* on this Psalm fittingly introduces his critical findings about the value of the histories. He fancies spectators assembled in the amphitheatre, the wrestling-ground for histrions and gladiators. The crowd will not emerge from this spectacle without damage to their sense of human dignity. But just as the sight of such vile performances will, as it were, impair our eyes and ears, they can be improved so as to perceive the divine truth, not by nature or medical art, but by the grace of Christ. [3]

In analyzing this text and correlating it to some other ones, we hope to show that by 1531 Erasmus had formed, if not an original conception of history, at least a definite opinion on the enthusiastic revaluation of history that was taking place everywhere and even within the circle of his close friends. His was no doubt a negative opinion; yet indifference and outspoken criticism were balanced by persistent meditation on the historical thought of the Christian fathers. Upon their pattern he formed his view of history, although some of his conclusions were highly original. His contemporaries, with few exceptions, seem to have ignored his thoughts on this subject; but then Erasmus, in turn, failed to support their historical endeavours.

There was at no period of Erasmus' life a lack of familiar books which could have stimulated his interest for history. Already Valla and Politian, two guiding stars of his adolescent years, clearly presented the essentials of the humanist approach to history. But Erasmus had no use for Valla's elegant adaptation of Thucydides' scientific pragmatism. He could never have repeated that history was superior to philosophy nor that everything recorded by historians, however repulsive the facts, was worthy of commem-

---

tis, nisi qui in Christum crucifixum intendit oculos (373DE). ... Huiusmodi rerum ac verborum varietas, quoties incidit in claris quidem sed tamen profanis rerum scriptoribus, accidit autem frequenter, fatemur, aut oblivione factum, aut inscitia, aut alio quopiam casu. Neque raro fit, ut inter varia narrantes nemo sit qui dicat verum. Quid mirum, quum nec illic quidem ubi maxime consentiunt, semper vera narrent? Absit autem ab animis Christianorum ut, si quando in sacris libris similis occurrat species, suspicentur oblivionem aut errorem Prophetae. Titus Livius, Thucydides, Herodotus, Plutarchus caeterique huius generis docti, facundi diligentesque fuerunt, sed quoniam nihil aliud erant quam homines, subinde falluntur et fallunt. At coelestis ille spiritus, cuius afflatu proditae sunt sacrae litterae, nec labi potest, nec fallere novit. Huic fundamento innixi, si qua species occurrat quae remoratur intellectum nostrum, posteaquam exploratum habuerimus nihil esse commissum incuria librariorum, existimabimus verborum dissonantia nostram oscitantiam excitari ac specie absurditatis nos admoneri, ut latens ibi mysterium scrutemur (378AB)"; cf. LB 1. 998A; *Opus epistolarum Des. Erasmi Roterodami*, ed. P.S. Allen etc., Oxford 1906ff., 10.171 (hereafter: Allen...).

[3] LB 5.369AB: "Qui sedent in amphitheatris, spectaturi gladiatorum paria aut histriones comoediam tragoediamve saltaturos, quoniam oculos et aureis adferunt talibus spectaculis dignas, e theatro fere discedunt se ipsis deteriores. Tales oculos, tales aureis si quis habet vestrum, oret Dominum ut ipsi dignetur impertiri oculos mundi cordis, quibus cernuntur spiritualia, aureis puras, quibus percipiuntur arcana coelestis sapientiae. Tales oculos, tales aureis nec nativitas dat nec medicorum ars: solus ille cuius spiritu renascimur, novatque totum hominem, tales oculos inserit animis nostris, tales aures addit spiritui nostro."

14

oration. [4]   Again it would be surprising if Erasmus did not carefully read the preface with which Politian introduced his edition of Suetonius, [5] for in 1518 Erasmus himself prepared Suetonius for Froben's press.   Resting on Cicero's moral and utilitarian criteria, Politian's text is an accomplished and memorable panegyric on history.   Erasmus' own preface, though famous and important, does not once recall Politian's ideas and certainly is no panegyric. [6]

At Paris young Erasmus was on friendly terms with two humanist historians, Robert Gaguin and Paulus Aemilius.   In 1495 he had the honour of contributing an elegant but otherwise rather insignificant letter to Gaguin's *De origine et gestis Francorum*. [7]   Aemilius later wrote a similar historical work, and Erasmus' correspondence shows some interest in it—only, however, until he was able to obtain a copy of the long delayed publication for his personal library. [8]   Whether, later on, he ever formed an opinion on the real value of the two histories we do not know.   While Erasmus resided in England, Thomas More was working on his *History of Richard III*. [9]   In his preserved writings Erasmus never referred to the work.   What a contrast to his reaction when More turned out *Utopia,* to the writing of which More may have sacrificed the completion of his historical study.   Another friend from the happy days in England was Polydore Vergil.   Erasmus twice persuaded Froben to print Vergil's *De inventoribus rerum,* [10] but never encouraged his *Historia Anglica,* a more sound and seriously historical undertaking.   On the contrary, Erasmus was anxious to call Vergil publicly back to his Greek studies which had suffered, as Vergil himself admitted, from his preoccupation with the *Historia*. [11]   The latter was not printed in Basel before Erasmus had left, and then the publisher was Bebel whom Erasmus distrusted. [12]

An intimate friend of Erasmus in the Basel period was Beatus Rhenanus, gifted with critical talent and a fine sense of historical proportions which left him a lone pillar of sound judgment amid the extravagant claims of Germany's humanist historians and patriots.   His sober views on the *translatio imperii,* for instance, may well bear the mark of Erasmus' influence. [13]   On the other hand, Erasmus remained perfectly cold in the

---

[4] L. Valla, *Opera omnia,* ed. E. Garin, 1.565ff., 2.5f.; cf. 1.561, 586.

[5] *Angeli Politiani opera,* Basel 1553, 499ff.

[6] Allen 2. 579ff.   In addition Erasmus probably knew Pontano's dialogue *Actius,* an important inquiry into the relation between history and poetry; cf. LB 1.1019E, 9.92E; Allen 2.99n., 6.474.

[7] Allen 1.149ff.

[8] Allen 2.479, 3.149, 203, 342.

[9] R.W. Chambers, *Thomas More,* London 1935, 115ff.; E.E. Reynolds, *Saint Thomas More,* London 1953, 80ff.

[10] Allen 4.426f., 430, 506, 5.542, 6.329.

[11] Allen 6.378f., 7.432.

[12] Cf. Allen 9.335, 362.

[13] P. Joachimsen, *Geschichtsauffassung* 125ff., 140ff.; for Erasmus' rejection of a more than nominal *translatio imperii*: Allen 2. 584f.

face of Rhenanus' outstanding historical work. He handed down an unmistakable warning to this friend when referring to the letters of Pope Pius II. Such epistolography, he said, is an undertaking even more dangerous than compiling contemporary history, full of bitter aloes, as Horace would say. [14] Years later, in 1526, Erasmus referred in almost slighting terms to Rhenanus' annotations to Pliny which, in the author's own opinion, presented an entirely new approach to palaeography. [15]

The crescendo of publications important for the study of history reached a climax in the years 1530-32. [16] The opening pages of Erasmus' own *Commentary on Psalm 33* form part of this flood and, however much the other contributions differed from one another, were likely intended to challenge them all. Erasmus ignored the first printed editions of Machiavelli's *Prince* and Carion's *Chronicon,* but he was dismayed—and for very good reasons, as we shall see—at that nonconformist and radical masterwork, Sebastian Franck's *Chronica, Zeytbuch und Geschychtbibel.* [17] At the same time Cornelius Agrippa's *De incertitudine et vanitate scientiarum* attracted his attention. Repugnant information about the author may have put him off before he managed to obtain a copy of the book which contained a vitriolic, but superficial, criticism of historiography as well as every other human enterprise. [18] Should he have read it, he surely must have felt that this was not the sort of humble doubt of human accomplishments which he himself preached in the *Praise of Folly* and eventually applied to history. Yet another friend and admirer of Erasmus published in 1531 his most important work. Vives' *De disciplinis* contains an original inquiry into the working of history based upon texts which Erasmus never bothered to analyze more fully, in particular Cicero's *De oratore* but probably also Politian's preface to Suetonius mentioned above. [19] Nor did Erasmus ever discuss the views of Vives and he may not have realized that Vives' grasp of the subject of history, in keeping with the whole book, was outstanding.

Erasmus, it would seem, considered his *Commentary* of 1531 to be his last word on the question of history. When in 1535 Sepulveda, the future historiographer of Charles V, accused him of certain inaccuracies in his geographical and historical facts, the old man seemed almost too ready to admit serenely and categorically: "*in locis et in historia crebro lapsus sum*". [20]

---

[14] Allen 4. 501; cf. 2. 582f., 4.514, 7.415.

[15] Allen 6.16f. (ed. n.), 6.281.

[16] Cf. A. Lhotsky, *Oesterreichische Historiographie,* Vienna 1962, 73f. Note especially the Haguenau reprint, under the title *Historiae encomium,* of Alciato's epistle dedicatory to his *Annotationes in Tacitum* (A. Alciato, *Le lettere,* Florence 1953, 220ff.) This text was known to Erasmus: LB 1.1011A.

[17] Allen 9.153 (ed.n.), 406, 410, 445 (ed.n.), 453f.

[18] Allen 9.351f.

[19] L. Vives, *Opera,* Basel 1555, 1.368ff., 504ff.

[20] Allen 10.393f., 11.13f. I could not check the *epistola ad Euagrium,* but twice in 1530 Erasmus located Constantinople correctly in Thracia (LB 3.1334A, 5.352B); there is also a correct reference to Rhegium previous to Sepulveda's accusations (LB 7.657f.).

II

Ultimately Erasmus would attempt to understand and define the place of history against the background of his religious convictions. First, however, he could not and did not avoid the confrontation with those more secular aspects of historical studies which his contemporaries knew largely from their reading of Cicero. Not that he ignored the value of historical knowledge as a school subject and a civic virtue, but rather his own findings in this direction may have seemed inconclusive, even to himself, and the rhetorical use of *exempla* taken from history, inevitable to him as to other humanists, only increased his doubt as to whether history could ever reveal the truth.

As the basic aim of education Erasmus once named "*cognito rerum ac verborum*".[21] "*Rerum et verborum varietas*", on the other hand, is the summary vice of which he accused history in the *Commentary on Psalm 33*.[22] Long before, for instance in the *Institutio principis Christiani* of 1516, he had warned of the dangerous influence of Herodotus and Xenophon, Sallust and Livy upon the youthful reader, since they exhibited examples of despotic, selfish, and arbitrary greatness.[23] It is not entirely inconsistent with this warning that Erasmus a year later published his own edition of Suetonius. In the preface to the dukes of the two Saxonies, responsible adults in this case, he emphasized the immense value of history to princes, only to proceed afterwards to a shattering lesson on human evils and princely vice uncovered by the thoughtful study of Roman history.[24]

Cicero and, after him, the early humanists of Italy and their German disciples had propagated the cult of Clio as an act of national awakening. This patriotic ideal was meaningless to Erasmus. It will later be shown that he became increasingly disillusioned with the leadership which secular princes could give to a bewildered and corrupted Christendom. Yet the hope he placed in them was never totally lost, nor was the wish quite abandoned that the thoughtful study of secular history would teach them a sobering and often shocking lesson.

For the problems involved in the rhetorical use of history Erasmus had a little more sympathy. The humanist, first and last, is a rhetorician, a linguist. His professional devotion as well as skill is aligned to *verba,* not to *res*. His real *gesta,* deeds, are *verba,* the words, and not *res gestae,* the actions of historical significance. To achieve the mastery of verbal

---

[21] LB 1.521A.
[22] LB 5.378A.
[23] LB 4.588AB; cf. LB 2.111B; Allen 6. 482.
[24] Allen 2.579ff.

expression a humanist professes the *artes liberales* and among them *historia rerum gestarum*. Theoretical systems never much bothered Erasmus, but basically he seems to have considered history and poetry as two cognate subjects of learning, both ancillary to grammar or the advanced stage of grammar, rhetoric, which relies upon either for its material. [25]

These, of course, were widely held views, and so were the principles upon which Cicero had hoped to found a national historiography worthy of the greatness of Rome. Not only *narratio,* had he said, but *exornatio* too is needed, for the effective structure (*exaedificatio*) which history is able to achieve lies both *in rebus et in verbis.* [26] Now this renders inevitable the crucial question about the relation between *res* and *verba,* between *fictio* and *veritas.* Indeed the implications could not be hidden from Cicero's mind. [27] Even if his famous "*concessum est rhetoribus ementiri in historiis*" was but a joke, [28] the need to distinguish between truth and legend and to achieve a balance between the double requirement of popular edification and adequate style, had been clear to Cicero as it had been clear to Livy and Sallust. These problems were known to Bruni and Valla, they stirred Pontano and Vives and even, albeit to a lesser degree, Politian, the aesthete.

In the light of this tradition must be interpreted the letter of homage which young Erasmus contributed to Gaguin's *Frankish History.* It demanded of the historian "*fides et eruditio*", veracity and erudition, that is, letters, the art of the rhetorician. Erasmus will occasionally repeat the request for truthfulness in historiography. [29] But it would seem more significant that already in the letter to Gaguin the achievement of *fides* depended on literary accomplishments. An author's *gravitas,* said Erasmus, adds to the trustworthiness of his material, while his *levitas* corrupts the truth innate in the facts. [30] But as the aging Erasmus grew increasingly doubtful of the value of all purely human achievements, the real depth which the problem of historical truth would assume for him became quite different from the dilemma of the Ciceronian tradition between fiction and fact, *verba* and *res.* Ultimately he felt called upon to distinguish between the fables of profane history and the truth of *historia sacra.* His disregard for the Ciceronian criteria must be understood as an act of faith.

De ratione studii, another opusculum of Erasmus' early days, contains a passage [31] emphasizing among other things the importance of "*historia*" in education. But of all "*historiographi*" only Valerius Maximus is mentioned by name, a typical collector of historical *exempla* in the rhetorical tradition,

---

[25] LB 1.514D, 523C-E, 5.853CD, 906EF; Allen 2.34, 6.194; cf. B. Weinberg, *A History of Literary Criticism in the Italian Renaissance,* Chicago 1960, 1.13ff.

[26] Cicero, *De oratore* 2.12.54, 2.15.63f.

[27] Cicero, *De legibus* 1.1.4.

[28] Cicero, *Brutus* 11.42; cf. M. Rambaud,*Cicéron et l'histoire romaine,* Paris 1952, 14f.

[29] Allen 7.103; Hieronymi vita, *Erasmi opuscula,* ed. W.K. Ferguson, The Hague 1933, lines 1-78 (hereafter: *Hieronymi vita...*); cf. LB 1.353C.

[30] Allen 1.150; cf. 7.101.

[31] LB 1.523E, 524D.

whom nobody today would rank with Livy and Tacitus. In all the genres of humanist writing there constantly occur references to the heroes of history along with those of mythology in such a way that alluding to a historical figure often yields no more than a figure of speech.

As will be shown in the second part of this study, Erasmus' scattered references to some historical character are normally consistent with each other, at least if one respects Erasmus' belief that human nature as such is fickle. Man, past and present, turns toward him a face which is so complex that often no true portrait can be painted. Rather contrasting features must be noted whenever the observer moves to a different point of view. This concept might seem singularly modern, were not Erasmus' biographical sketches to show that even a complex character was perfectly static to him. There occurs no real change in a man's life-span; the passing of years will but gradually unfold his true nature. [32]

III

From what has been said so far, it should be clear why Erasmus would occasionally try his hand in biography, but never be a historian. For one thing, he lacked the stimulus of Beatus Rhenanus' patriotism. This is true of other humanists such as Vives. But Vives, who wrote remarkable pages about secular history, was helped by his strong belief in human progress which implied the usefulness of history if only the truth could be established in a satisfactory way. And in order to do so Vives could avail himself of the tools of dialectic. In contrast, Erasmus was not very successful at handling problems dialectically, even if he had shared Vives' belief in human progress. We must now show how completely he failed to share this belief. Only so can we understand why he needed, and found, very different means to master the problems of history, of man's place in history, and of verbal expression to render historical facts.

Erasmus was hardly the writer to shun commonplaces, yet he must be singled out from his entire surroundings for never having repeated Cicero's torrential exclamation: *"historia vero testis temporum, lux veritatis, vita memoriae, magistra vitae, nuntia vetustatis..."*. [33] Not that he doubted the usefulness of the single example chosen from history; but how could he have accepted a statement that clearly valued secular history as a system, a method? It seemed to him that even the individuals in history kept changing

---

[32] Cf. below pp. 23f., 69ff.

[33] Cicero, *De oratore* 2.9.36; nor could I trace in Erasmus any obvious reminiscences of *De oratore* 2.15.62f. or *Orator* 34.120.

faces, as it were, and therefore he never tried to mould his biographical sketches into pieces of coherent history. Especially *lux veritatis* would seem incompatible with Erasmus' ideas. Human history most emphatically was not the avenue by which truth could be arrived at. The conquest of truth, or perhaps some facets of truth, depended upon the right time rather than the factfinding of skilled historians. Hence Erasmus' views are better rendered by another saying of classical antiquity which acquired, partly through the *Adagia,* considerable influence on thought and art: *veritas filia temporis.*

From Bruno to the Enlightenment, the image of truth, as the daughter of time, has suggested the idea of historical progress. [34] Time, in this case *chronos,* not *kairos,* gradually brings to light the truth which therefore is bound to be known in an ever more complete form. When showing many of the somersaults to which the meaning of *veritas filia temporis* was subjected in the course of its frequent repetitions, F. Saxl referred to Mary Tudor who used the motto as a personal device in her crest of arms, on her state seal and coinage: "Time was fulfilled and had brought with it Truth, long banished from the realm". [35] Here the birth of truth from time is seen as a unique, accomplished act,—and as such Mary's interpretation would swiftly be confuted by subsequent events. Here too time is *chronos,* the lapse of time, development in time. What these interpretations emphasize is the progress of truth, whether partial and gradual as for Vives, Bruno, and Bacon, or total as for Mary Tudor. None leaves a way back from truth to error, from light to obscurity.

Erasmus' view on the interrelation between truth and time can be learned from two *adagia,* "Tempus omnia revelat" and "Nosce tempus". Only in special cases does Erasmus use the *Adagia* for the expression of his own opinion; on the whole, the manual is a monumental quarry of classical thought and expression made available for everyday usage. The arrangement of the *adagium* "Tempus omnia revelat", however, is no doubt very elaborate. It is there that Erasmus quotes the saying *veritas filia temporis,* [36] but his own interpretation in two points strikingly contrasts with the ones just mentioned.

For one thing, although the classic expression *veritas filia temporis* renders the central idea of the *adagium,* the fatherhood of the pagan god Time, Erasmus prefers for his title an utterly unremarkable *tempus omnia revelat* whose chief merit probably was that it could be plucked from the work of a Christian father. [37] A variety of classical quotations follow,

---

[34] G. Gentile, *Giordano Bruno e il pensiero del Rinascimento,* Florence 1920, 87-111; cf. E. Garin, *Medievo e Rinascimento,* ²Bari 1961, 195ff. ("La storia nel pensiero del Rinascimento").

[35] F. Saxl, Veritas filia temporis, *Philosophy and History,* Essays presented to E. Cassirer, ed. R. Klibansky and H.J. Paton, Oxford 1936, 207f. and passim.

[36] LB 2.527F-528E; the quotation comes, together with other material used in this *adagium,* from Aulus Gellius 12.11.

[37] Tertullian, *Apologeticum* 7.13.

showing Saturn (*Kronos*=*chronos*) as the father of a daughter named Truth; but towards the end, as if to avert an inherent, though unmentioned danger, the pagan images of Time's fathership are broken up for the sake of Christ's words in Matthew 10.26: "*nihil enim est opertum quod non revelabitur, et occultum quod non scietur*".

The door is ostensibly kept open for the reader to realize that a Christian interpretation of the classical pagan dictum is possible, and no doubt it would have to be either the anagogical one that not any time reveals the truth but only the *tempus ultimum* of man's history or, allegorically, the "*seculum Christianum*" [38] of Christ's everlasting presence. Saturn may indeed stand as a *figura* for Christ, either the Lord of the Last Judgment or the teacher of the true Christians of all times.

In the same *adagium* a second point must be noted. Some of Erasmus' quotations do not emphasize so much that what time brings to light is necessarily the truth, but simply that it reveals what has been hidden and changes what exists. This is particularly so with two verses from Sophocles' *Ajax*:

> Time in its slow, illimitable course
> Brings all to light and buries all again. [39]

This and other quotations merely suggest an all-embracing process of mutation and are incompatible with the ideas of a gradual progress or final breakthrough of truth. Immediately before the final quotation from Seneca there is a line from Livy according to which truth is often hard pressed, though never quite extinguished. [40] It is on such a note of reserve that Erasmus ends the *adagium*.

Erasmus also develops his own way to talk about the children of time and his metaphors are at complete variance with the happy expectations of his youth. Then he had spoken of a world progressing toward its Golden Age, but now, in 1530, he writes to Melanchthon the sad, ironical words: "*hoc saeculum nobis peperit Evangelium*". [41] This must be understood in the light of a similar remark to the same Melanchthon seven years earlier: "*genuit olim Evangelium novum genus hominum mundo,* but what sort of creatures the 'Gospel' is producing now, one would rather not mention". [42] To Ammonius he writes in 1531: "*mundus iamdudum abortit, quando sit vitalem partum aediturus nescio...*". In this case the typical continuation of Erasmus' thought is made explicit: but Christ is alive; he, the *choragus*, will bring this hopeless play to its wholesome *catastrophe*. [43] Thus Erasmus'

---

[38] See below p. 38.
[39] Sophocles. *Ajax* 646f., F. Storr's translation.
[40] Livy 22.39.19; Erasmus does not follow the now commonly accepted reading, but prefers with Valla the more obscure: "a veritate laborare nimis saepe aiunt, exstingui nunquam". Livy's context, however, permits no doubt as to the meaning.
[41] Allen 9.13.
[42] Allen 5.595; cf. LB 10.1257E (*Hyperaspistes* I): "Tale seculum, Luthere, nobis peperit tua fortitudo...".
[43] Allen 9.257.

thought wanders from the earthly abode of secular Time and his illgotten children to the higher plane of *historia sacra.*

With the Latin term *tempus* Erasmus renders not only the Greek *chronos,* but often also kairos, the right moment, which is infinitely more relevant to his own emotional approach to time and timeliness. To *kairos* he dedicates the *adagium "Nosce tempus".* He realizes that 'opportunity' or 'occasion' might be more sensible translations for the Greek term; they would, however, destroy the direct, visible notion of *Kairos,* the god, whose feet glide over the rotating wheel and whose front is covered with curly hair, while the back of his head is bald. He is a most bizarre, elementary power "which turns the honest man to dishonesty, damage to profit, pleasure to bother, good deeds to bad ones and vice versa, in short, which changes the nature of everything." [44]

This formidable creature reminds one of Machiavelli's *Fortuna* who is an equally plastic expression of the same allegory. But the Florentine's bolder interpretation is not considered by Erasmus. Machiavelli's *Fortuna* will forever defy who runs after her, but the rare virtuoso who dares to brave her from the front might catch the woman and "beat her into submission". [45] Erasmus' more conventional explanation only knows of one actor, *Kairos* himself. Either he bows his head towards you so that you may hold on to his hair, or he flees from you and you will never catch him.

In this *adagium* Erasmus limits himself to quotations from pagan antiquity and Politian and to his usual explanatory comments. How the myth of the pagan god *Kairos* fits into his own Christian approach to time, he does not say. We cannot here discuss Erasmus' concept of fortune, but we may be sure that he could never have subscribed to Valla's elusive, but essentially antichristian definition of *fortuna*: "*nihil aliud est quam deus qui moderatur omnia aut ipsius dei moderatio*". [46] When Erasmus once calls *kairos* the most efficient cure for things incurable, [47] he is pointing in direction of the *Praise of Folly* where Fortune, under the name of *Rhamnusia,* but sketched by Holbein with her traditional emblems, appears in sisterly concord with Folly. [48] As *Moria,* the light-hearted goddess of pagan parentage, becomes by way of paradox the eloquent preacher of Christian virtue, so the pagan god *Kairos,* that whimsical fellow, may well end up as the chosen instrument of Providence. This at least would seem the implication when even Erasmus' edition of the *New Testament* emphasizes in a note that the term *kairos* must be interpreted in the light of its divinity with the Greeks, rather than being taken as a mere species of the genus *chronos.* [49]

---

[44] LB 2.289f.

[45] F. Chabod, *Machiavelli and the Renaissance,* transl. D. Moore, London 1958, 146; cf. W. Kaegi, *Chronica mundi,* Einsiedeln 1954, 36.

[46] L. Valla, *Opera,* ed. Garin, 1.567.

[47] Allen 9.91.

[48] LB 4.486.

[49] LB 6.436DE.

Erasmus, then, knows of two ways by which time may uncover the truth. Some truths are suddenly revealed to us in moments of inspiration; the full Truth will come to light at the fulfilment of time. Neither way lends itself to systematic digging into history and chronology. If it were to be relied upon, history must be very different from the sort of investigations to which that term would normally refer in Erasmus' day as in our own.

IV

We may now approach the fundamental problems which, for Erasmus, overshadow the relation between the historical fact and its verbal expression and determine the meaning of the word *historia* in his usage.

In a famous passage of the *Convivium religiosum* Erasmus examines the true criteria of saintliness which do not always ring out from the 'catalogue' of the official saints. The rigid standards of frigid theology cannot restrict the true spirit. Erasmus would much rather let the entire works of Duns Scotus and a few more of his kind perish than the writings of Cicero and Plutarch. What could sound holier in the ears of a Christian than the words of the dying Socrates, a man who so distrusted his own deeds ("*facta*") that he could humbly conceive the hope that leads to salvation. "*Sancte Socrates, ora pro nobis*", Erasmus cannot suppress the exclamation. [50] But a few years later this same Erasmus grumbles in *Ciceronianus*: how can quotations from Socrates and Plato add greater weight and majesty to our speech than Solomon's Proverbs or Christ's words in the Gospel? Must we be offended by the books inspired by the Holy Spirit rather than by Homer, Euripides and Ennius? Rather let us refrain from mentioning the Holy Ghost in this context, lest we compare things divine with things human. *History* which cannot be trusted does not even deserve the *name of history*. In this way let us compare Moses, the historian, with Herodotus, the story-teller, the history of the Pentateuch with the fables of Diodorus. Whether one considers the authors or the topics, there is just no similarity. [51]

It may be argued that one is here faced with the unbridgeable gulf between the young Erasmus and the old one, the heir of Renaissance humanism and the contemporary of the Reformation. To some degree this gulf is undeniable, but does it really extend to Erasmus' understanding of history? As there is only one Solomon, lusty and criminal, peace-loving and saintly, [52] there is only one Socrates; Erasmus still calls him "*sanctus*" in

---

[50] LB 1.682A-683E.
[51] LB 1.997E-998B.
[52] LB 1.418E, 5.228CD, 299E; Allen 2.83, 206.

1531. [53] There is only one Socrates, only one set of historical facts, but there is more than one understanding. In history all depends on whether we look at it the right way. This is what in Erasmus' view makes history dangerous, for right and wrong must change according to circumstances.

In the *Hieronymi vita* Erasmus states "that in the opinion of Socrates nobody will lie more aptly than he who speaks the truth most adroitly". From the viewpoint of literary skill, truth and lie complement each other smoothly. As evidence Erasmus cites the histories of Herodotus and Xenophon. [54] Thus *Historia,* the discipline of the skilful scholars and rhetoricians, tends to become *fabula* as it involves flattering and lying, especially when the historian looks at the events of his own day. *Fabula,* on the other hand, may reveal an abyss of truth whenever a story, whether creditable or not, conceals within itself *historia mystica* [55] and the Holy Spirit enlightens a man to understand the sense of its allegories.

The *Commentary on Psalm 33* remarks on the subject of David's feigned insanity in front of Abimelech: "by the way, as for the bare recording of facts (*"rerum gestarum nudam commemorationem"*), similar cases may be read in the profane histories", such as the pretended insanity of Ulysses or the feigned idiocy of Junius Brutus. But "far be it from any Christian to think that [David's case] here is just the simple account of actual events (*rerum gestarum simplicem historiam*), for what happened here did not happen by chance, but God's special injunction." [56]

That Moses erected the serpent's cross in the wilderness is perfectly true history, but it is not just *historia* as one could believe, had not Christ himself in John 3.14 opened this *figura* of Numbers. In the same way Erasmus will attempt the explanation of Psalm 33: "so far I have presented but the shell of the nut, and thus you have only tasted the husk of the barley ; I just showed you Silenus. If God deigns to help us, we shall now extract the kernel, expose the fine flour, and expound Silenus." [57] In view of such mysteries the antithesis between Christian thought and pagan expression is completely removed. Erasmus gladly submits to the spell of the fine classical symbol of Silenus. What is more, the same symbol, used here exegetically rather than historically, can be found much earlier in Erasmus' *adagium* "*Sileni Alcibiadis*" and there it is projected into the truly historical dimension. Socrates and Antisthenes, Diogenes and Epictetus, Christ and John the Baptist, the Apostles and finally the bishops of old, such as Martin of Tours, they all succeeded each other in embodying Silenus, while great

---

[53] Allen 9.132.

[54] *Hieronymi vita* 43ff.: "Quodquidem iuxta Socratis sententiam, nemo sit ad mentiendum accomodatior quam qui ad vera dicendum est appositissimus, quod eiusdem artificis partes esse ducat, certissime veridicum esse et nihil omnino veri dicere. Hoc quidem consilio suam historiam contexuit Herodotus, hac ratione Xenophon Cyri descripsit institutionem, non ad historiae fidem, sed ad exemplum probi principis."

[55] Ibid. 1-78; LB 5.372E.

[56] LB 5.371AB.

[57] LB 5.371DE, 370Eff.; cf. 5.869E: *historia in specie absurda* recommended to the preacher.

24

princes and prelates were often 'inverted' Sileni, hollow underneath the shining surface. [58]

In the *adagium* of Silenus, as elsewhere in Erasmus' work, the climate of Renaissance Platonism is unmistakable. [59] The human body has its dignity—it is "holier than 600 consecrated loaves [60]"—, but its dignity, the dignity of Adam, stems from harbouring the "New Adam", Paul's *nova creatura*. [61] The analysis of history in the *Commentary on Psalm 33* takes its origin from the *discrimen inter corpus et animam*. [62] History, which is man's history, is true only if it can spot the interior man, the Silenus. Erasmus' approach continues the dualistic concept of history from Augustine to Otto of Freising, but more precisely, as focused on the individual rather than the aggregate, it initiates the historical vision of Sebastian Franck and the Baptists. In the case of Franck the *adagium* "*Sileni Alcibiadis*" marks not only the guiding principle of his entire historical vision; directly or indirectly, it provides the *leitmotiv* for two of his finest books. [63]

The reader will have noticed that in many of the above quotations Erasmus uses the term *historia* in that sense which was customary in Scriptural exegesis throughout the Middle Ages. One might argue that to Erasmus *historia* is the Latin expression for two different things: that when referring to secular historiography he is, like Herodotus, thinking of a critical inquiry into facts both past and present, whereas when referring to the Bible he uses *historia* to mean "the literal sense". This is not so. The two notions could coincide in terminology because both reflected the same human attitude. The understanding of history always demanded investigation as well as interpretation. If these were directed towards *Historia Sacra* rather than secular history, the dignity of the undertaking would grow, but the technique would not necessarily change. Erasmus cannot allegorize the *historia* of Psalm 33 without repeated side-glances at such historiographers as Livy. Like scores of Christian authors before him, Erasmus really puts Herodotus and Moses on one level: their accounts might completely differ in trustworthiness, but each wrote history and thus became a source for subsequent historical inquiry, whether theological or humanist. We have quoted already Erasmus' statement in *Ciceronianus* that "history, divorced from faith, does not even deserve the name of history". *Nomen historiae*, this refers not to technicalities, but to a positive and comprehensive science.

---

[58] LB 2.770ff.; cf. 4.428AB; E. Wind, *Pagan Mysteries in the Renaissance*, London 1958, 143ff., 176ff. and on art: 71, 85n., to which could be added Holbein's sketch of Silenus among the illustrations to the *Praise of Folly*; W. Kaiser, *Praisers of Folly*, Cambridge Mass. 1963, especially 54ff., 245; cf. M. de Montaigne, *Essais* 3.12 (beginning).

[59] E.g. LB 5.38F-39A.

[60] LB 5.370AB; cf. 1.770Cff.

[61] LB 5.15-17, 44Ff., 84E.

[62] LB 5.369A.

[63] S. Franck, *Paradoxa*, ed. H. Ziegler, Jena 1909, already in the introduction (5-12) there occur some obvious reminiscences of Erasmus' *Commentary on Psalm 33* and the *adagium* "*Sileni Alcibiadis*"; on *Chronica, Zeytbuch...* 3.3 (Chronick von den Romischen kätzern) see below p. 50; cf. W. Kaegi, *Chronica mundi* 43ff.

V

Another strand in Erasmus' thought will help us to understand his concept of *historia*: *theatrum mundi*. The world is a stage; man acts his preordained part until the play is done. Erasmus was fascinated with this immortal theme and frequently referred to it when meditating about history. In the opening pages of his *Commentary on Psalm 33* we found his essential thoughts on the nature of history which, one remembers, were introduced by the image of the stage. History, like the play on the stage, shapes the receptive faculties of its audience. The morals of the spectator will be impaired or improved according to the quality of the performance.

Best known among Erasmus' frequent borrowings from the accessories of the theatre is the term *tragoedia* in reference to the Lutheran Reformation. J. Huizinga once noted that Erasmus did not actually mean a 'tragedy' in our modern sense, but a 'spectacle'. [64] In fact Erasmus' usage of the word is hardly less emotive than our own, but he never detached it from its liaison with the stage. Moreover, he closely related to each other *tragoedia* and *comoedia,* the tragic performance and the comic one. With Oecolampadius' wedding the *"Lutherana tragoedia"* suddenly became a *"comoedia"*. [65] Thus, as an *adagium* has it, 'comedy' and 'tragedy' are composed of the same letters. [66]

What matters to us at this point is that the stage, with its tragic and comic plays, is almost identical with the world of *fabula*. *Fabula,* as we have seen, is either opposed to or, interpreted allegorically, conducive to true *historia*. The term *fabula* repeatedly refers to plays performed on the stage and would seem particularly suitable whenever Erasmus wished to avoid the words *tragoedia* or *comoedia*. After all the play was still in progress and its final definition must depend upon the last scene. [67]

Not only is the reference to the stage as such an obvious allegory, the play itself, whatever its temper and topic, is a fable, a mystery-play. There can be no doubt as to the set of allegories: the stage is the world, the *choragus* is Christ, the plot is history, the acts and scenes its various phases. Historical events, despite the breathtaking actuality of, say, the Reformation, are ultimately not real but symbolic of a happening beyond all limits of time

---

[64] J. Huizinga, *Erasmus* (German trans. by W. Kaegi) 4 Basel 1951, 162n. (the note is not contained in the English translations); cf. Allen 1.52, 4.481, 499, 7.164, 8.226, 9.96; often the reference is to Erasmus' personal part in the play: e.g. LB 1.992EF, also noticeable for expressing the confusion that may accompany the idea of *theatrum historiae*: "quocunque me verto, video mutata omnia, in alio sto proscenio, aliud conspicio theatrum, imo mundum alium."

[65] Allen 7.369.

[66] LB 2.823F; cf. Allen 9.112f., 224, 315.

[67] Allen 4.575, 6.275, 8.89, 9.208, 257; LB 4.428BC, 10.1579D.

and space. The actor is an allegory for man, but man in history, as we saw, is again the symbol for the inner man. Historical man—and often Erasmus himself is the actor—must perform in the *fabula,* the play; this is his functional purpose: *"aut opportet tragoedias omneis agere aut insanire",* [68] either you keep performing or you go mad. But the play will come to an end. Then man will be free to leave the stage of history and live his own *alter ego* in the sphere of truth. We may quote here again the words Erasmus wrote to Ammonius in 1531: " far too long already the world has been in labour; when it will give birth to a child fit to live, I do not know. So far the *proemia* [the first parts of the play] do not seem promising to me. But Christ is alive and directs the scenes of human affairs with his secret guidance. For the rest and until that *choragus* will produce the *catastrophe* [final act] of the play (*fabula*) I must continue to act in this play of life..." [69]

Only the *catastrophe* of the mystery-play will reveal the meaning of history, but as a Christian Erasmus knows what it is going to be. Time and again he expresses his unfailing hope for Christ to act as a *deus ex machina.* When all human actors are thrown into the most helpless confusion, he will intervene and lead the play to its salutary conclusion. [70]

The association of the term *historia* with the world of the stage has been credited to the Christian fathers and, in particular, to two passages of Tertullian which relate the Ciceronian terms *argumenta* and *historia* to mimic performances and, of course, sharply censure the amphitheatre. [71] Erasmus knew Tertullian's *Apologeticum* well; even though the passage in his *Commentary on Psalm 33* is directly inspired by Origen and, to a lesser degree, by Chrysostom. [72] In the wake of this patristic tradition an Isidore could conclude that *histrio* may philologically be derived from *historia,* [73] but in medieval chronicles the idea of *theatrum historiae* would seem surprisingly rare. In touching it passingly, Otto of Freising may have adapted a sentence by Eusebius [74] John of Salisbury, on the other hand, quoted in his *Policraticus* a passage by Petronius and thereupon developed the idea that life is play and play is life. He dealt with it at considerable length and with such depth that he could not fail to apply it to history as well. [75]

---

[68] LB 2.759E.

[69] Allen 9.257; cf. LB 1.746D: "videtis iam inverti mundi scenam; aut deponenda est persona, aut agendae sunt suae cuique partes".

[70] e.g. LB 2.52Fff.; Allen 4.481, 6.353, 7.53, 61f., 162, 164, 8.70, 89, 226, 9.224.

[71] K. Keuck, *Historia, Geschichte des Wortes...in der Antike und in den romanischen Sprachen,* Emsdetten 1934, 31; cf. Tertullian, *Apologeticum* 15.4, and *Ad nationes* 1.10 (Migne P.L. 1.647).

[72] Cf. LB 8.152ff. especially 153A (translation of a passage from Chrysostom's *Homilies* which Erasmus published in 1533. Both, Chrysostom's context and purpose, however, are different); for Origen's text which inspired Erasmus more directly see below n. 142.

[73] Isidore, *Etymologiae* 18.48; cf. K. Keuck, *Historia* 95.

[74] Otto of Freising, *Chronica sive historia de duobus civitatibus,* ed. W. Lammers, Darmstadt 1960, 4, 759 (Index s.v. tragedia); Eusebius 1.8.4.

[75] John of Salisbury, *Policraticus* 3.7.10; cf. E.R. Curtius, *European Literature and the Latin Middle Ages,* transl. W.R. Trask, New York 1953, 138ff.

To some degree the dramatical meaning of the term *historia* may have been suggested to the fathers by the dramatic historiography of Tacitus and the historical drama flourishing in his day, just as, later on, the monastic usage of the term *historia* for certain tropes bequeathed that name to more developed types of liturgical and secular drama. [76]

In Erasmus' own day the symbolism of *theatrum historiae* was employed, though not frequently, by other humanists as well. Budé had used it even before Erasmus' *Commentary* of 1531, though the latter may not have noticed this. Similar references occur repeatedly in Budé's later and more mature writings. [77] With the new generation of Patrizi and Baudouin, [78] *theatrum historiae,* with all the confusing relativism which that idea could ignite, succeeded as a fashionable, incessantly repeated cliché and an unintentional admission of mental imbalance in early modern Europe. Erasmus thus stands not alone amid the tradition of *theatrum historiae.* But he certainly stands out for expressing, humbly but with finality, his personal commitment to the historical events past and present.

VI

Whoever looks at the stream of history, this endless sequel of past events inextricably connected with the present, his first impression must be one of confusion. Erasmus too knew the "inexhaustible sea" in which the human individual is "just a bubble". [79] In a letter to Warham he likened human affairs to a sea, not one of the more stagnant ones but rather the Euripus which by day and by night withdraws seven times and rushes back just as often with incredible speed. [80] Such is also the flux of history: *nihil novum sub sole* was true in the days of Ecclesiastes and holds even truer today. [81] Or again, "up and down goes the flux of human affairs", but the general tendency is from bad to worse: "it is the nature of all human affairs that they deteriorate, relapse and degenerate, unless we resist, struggling with hand and foot". [82]

---

[76] K. Keuck, *Historia* 21f., 31f., 78ff., 97f.; cf. K. Young, *The Drama of the Medieval Church,* Oxford 1933.

[77] G. Budé, *De contemptu rerum fortuitarum,* Paris 1525(?), e.g. 30; *De philologia,* Paris 1532, 99; *De transitu Hellenismi ad Christianismum,* Paris 1535, 5, 30f., 33, 97, 99f.; cf. J. Bohatec, *Budé und Calvin,* Graz 1950, 283f.; cf. also Vives' *Fabula de homine* (1518).

[78] F. Patrizi, *Della Historia diece dialoghi,* Venice 1560, 1, 49f.; F. Baudouin, *De institutione historiae universae...,* passim (I used the reprint in *Artis historicae penus,* Basel 1579).

[79] See the *adagia 'Mare exhauris'* and *'Homo bulla',* LB 2.908AB, 500ff.

[80] Allen 5.561, cf. 5.155 and LB 2.357A-D.

[81] Allen 7.120.

[82] Allen 2.184, 581.

28

This first, depressing view of history may be overcome, if the flux of events is, as it were, directed into man-made channels, if facts are bundled into distinctive categories and chronological periods. Since Augustine, scores of Christian writers had balanced their low opinion of the human nature with profound admiration for God's redemptive plan wrought into the pattern of universal history. Often from a less religious standpoint, 16th century humanists were tackling afresh the systematic periodization of universal history. Erasmus, however, had no systematic vein; to him historical "*mutationes*", [83] by which periods may be marked off from each other, were of an elementary, cataclysmic nature. They were interventions by a super-human power, the *numen* or the *deus ex machina*. Hence he maintained a reserved attitude towards the conventions of historical periodization, even though they proved too convenient to be completely disposed of.

Erasmus' approach to history cannot be assessed in terms of a conflict between the cyclic and the linear conceptions. [84] Although he did at times employ some conventional pattern of successive historical ages, he did this so sparingly that the extent to which he could free himself of the common-places of historical thought in his day is all the more noticeable.

Of all conventional constructions of history Erasmus completely ignored the astrological cycles. Throughout his work he was opposed, not to some elementary knowledge, but to the serious study of astronomy and astrology. Not that he thought the science of the stars wrong or incompatible with the Christian faith, he simply felt it could not contribute to the real task of his generation, least of all to that contemplation of history which he wished to encourage. [85]

Erasmus cared little more for the protean theory of four world empires. There are casual hints to it in his letters, but the point he wished to make is nowhere a historical one. What, he once asked, if the evils of this time were such that the heavenly doctor felt compelled to use scalpel and fire rather than patches and ointment? What if God made a horrible use of Luther ("*voluit abuti Luthero*"), as he had made before of the Pharaohs and Philistines, Nebuchadnezzars and Romans? For God's particular intervention is manifested by the fact that sordid culprits and fools are allowed to play such an important part in this *fabula*. [86] In much the same vein Erasmus also indicted "the kingdom of monks and fools" as a providential number five to the kingdoms of the Assyrians and Greeks, Medes and Romans. [87]

It would seem a little more tempting for Erasmus to view the development of the Church as a sequence of consecutive phases, yet such views too

---

[83] E.g. Allen 5.77.
[84] M.P. Gilmore (*Humanists and Jurists* 108ff.) makes such a distinction.
[85] Cf. LB 4.509E, 543C, 7.8Eff., 9.214C, 10.1695CD; Allen 5.177.
[86] Allen 5.605; cf. below p. 77, n. 107.
[87] Allen 9.277; cf. J.H.J. van der Pot, *De periodisering der geschiedenis,* The Hague 1951, 78 etc. All that the structural divisions of Roman history are worth to Erasmus is an occasional side-glance, cf. Allen 3.138f., 4.181.

find only scarce and casual expression. The *Ratio verae theologiae* of 1518 distinguished five *tempora* determined by the churchman's outlook: the age before Christ, the age of Advent, dominated by John the Baptist, the age of Christ, the Apostles and Evangelists, the age of the established Church, characterized by secular protection, material wealth and new laws which did not always agree with Christ's commandments, and, finally, the age of outright degeneration. Erasmus, however, hastened to admit that such chronological categories might rather confuse the reader and forthwith dropped the matter. [88]

Without attempting a proper periodization of history, Erasmus frequently recalled the conventional pattern of three successive laws, beginning with the law of Nature, followed by the Mosaic law of Works, and completed by the Gospel law of Faith. [89] However, there is a puzzling and rather unique paragraph in the *Ecclesiastes* of 1535, presenting four ages of the law ("*legis tempora quatuor*") in a historical order. First comes God's own law in the earthly Paradise: ye shall not eat. This is counteracted by Satan's law: eat and be like God. Satan's commandment apparently is a sort of anti-law and therefore not included in the enumeration. Second comes the "exile" which lasts many centuries and knows only "the law of Nature, not yet as greatly obscured by vice as it would become as time went by". More detailed consideration is given to the third and fourth ages, dominated by Moses' old law and Christ's new one. [90] The implication no doubt is that every new law comes as an addition which does not invalidate the earlier ones. One is left in doubt about the origins of this unusual periodization. It can be related to Erasmus' own meditation of the various laws in the course of his continued brooding over Paul's epistle to the Romans. Though never prominent, a historical order of subsequent laws is repeatedly implied both in Erasmus' own comments on *Romans* as in those of Origen who guided him. [91] If Erasmus stated explicitly that no other age would follow the one of Christ, he may have wished to uphold the common patristic view, lest the reader be misled by some form of Joachism or a misinterpretation of Origen's eschatology.

We have been unable to find in Erasmus' writings any more substantial evidence on periodization and, therefore, must allow the conclusion that his

---

[88] LB 5.86-88.

[89] Two lines in *Commentary on Psalm 33* emphasize continuity rather than periodization: "Sub lege Naturae, sub lege Mosaica, sub Evangelii gratia, ab exordio mundi usque ad consummationem, incessanter Ecclesia benedicit Dominum..." (LB 5.388F); cf. LB 9.1222A-D, 10.1325f.

[90] LB 5.1075A-1077B.

[91] Cf. below p. 44. Ch. Bigg (*The Christian Platonists of Alexandria*, 2Oxford 1913, 250) writes: "Looking back over history Origen distinguished three separate progressive revelations of God, the Natural Law, the Law of Moses, and the Gospel. A fourth is still to come. It is the Eternal Gospel." This suggests the idea of a historical sequence, perhaps not fully borne out by passages in *De principiis* (P.G. 11.397f.) and *Comment. in Rom.* (2.8ff.; 3.6,9; and especially 6.8; P.G. 14, 890ff., 938ff., 955, 1076ff.) Typically, Origen pays no more attention to the periodization of history than Erasmus does. Cf. also R.C.P. Hanson, *Allegory and Event*, London 1959, 298.

condoning of the more conventional periodizations of history weighs lightly when compared with their popularity in the 16th century. Even the 'Renaissance' conception of a Golden Age followed by decay and rebirth was gradually abandoned or, at least, remoulded by him, as we shall attempt to show in the following section.

It has, however, often been noted that Erasmus could sense in a subtle way what seemed to give a moment in history its touch of originality. In particular his ability to understand a literary composition as the document of a given historical situation is remarkable, although basically applied to advancing philology rather than history. A well known instance is his warning that an ancient author, in this case Origen, must not be singled out for arbitrary judgment based on contemporary attitudes. Erasmus invites the readers to imagine for a moment that they were the contemporaries of Origen and were to consider Thomas Aquinas as the isolated representative of another age. "Who could bear him measuring the dogmas of the Church with the yardsticks (*gnomones*) of Aristotle and Averroes? Now that the Church is seen to have her infancy, youth, adulthood, perhaps also her old age [one notes how casually, just for the sake of the argument, the structural concept is referred to],...some would nevertheless treat the writings of all authors as if they belonged to the present time...". [92]

Analogous statements have been cited to prove that Erasmus possessed a 'modern' notion of development, but rarely dared to apply it, for instance, to Church history. According to this opinion he would have relapsed into static 'medieval' thought for fear of being associated with heretics and innovators. [93] How valid are such conclusions? We shall try to find out by investigating, in some detail, Erasmus' use of the 'Renaissance' pattern.

VII

As a humanist, Erasmus was bound to recognize the structural division of history into Antiquity, Middle Ages, and Renaissance. In particular his predictions of an imminent Golden Age of peace, piety, and culture have won a disproportionate celebrity with later generations and somehow established him as a key witness for the 'Renaissance' conception of history. In view of his basically doubtful attitude towards human progress, the blissful expectation of a Golden Age seems rather illogical. There were specific circumstances which led Erasmus to conceive this lofty dream, but

---

[92] Allen 7.102; cf. LB 1.992EF (transl. in M.P. Gilmore, *Humanists and Jurists* 103); LB 9.1219-21; 10.1546BC.

[93] E.g. S.A. Nulli, *Erasmo e il Rinascimento* esp. 247.

more significant is the long and slow process by which he afterwards adjusted it to his general understanding of history. Therefore, we must now look at his references to the Golden Age before we can locate this culminating period within the wider frame of his 'Renaissance' conception.

In Erasmus' earliest letters the concept of the Renaissance was manifest, the revival being one comprehensive action absorbing the efforts of the earlier Italian as well as Northern humanists and extending to Erasmus' own generation. [94] But as time went by, Erasmus' first unequivocal impression was complicated by several doubts. For one thing, he convinced himself that his own direct contemporaries among the Italian humanists could not really fill the boots of their predecessors, the great generation of Valla, Barbaro, and Politian, whom the young monk of Steyn had worshipped. [95] Moreover, he grew more resentful of a dangerous paganism which, he believed, was paramount in Italian humanism. [96] The result was the concept of a Golden Age, a concept formed to express the special hopes and endeavours of the Christian humanists in the north, a program for the future, and an ideal to which the Italians had never risen.

Still in 1515 Erasmus nostalgically mentioned a "Golden Age' as a vain dream of personal ease. [97] Soon afterwards, however, he expressed his hope for a future reflowering of all *bonae artes* when complimenting the new Pope Leo X. [98] There followed the famous visions of the Golden Age as a real achievement or near-achievement, sponsored by the peace-loving princes and crowned by the religious revival. [99] This concept was perhaps not fully established before 1517 and it cannot be said to have survived the second decade of the century. For then came the renewal of wars, the Lutheran Reformation, and the crescendo of attacks upon Erasmus from various camps. In the earlier 1520's a new, nostalgic vision of the Renaissance was expressed. The well known letter in 1523 to Gaverius (printed together with *Exomologesis*) was really a great obituary not so much of one common friend as of an entire brilliant generation of unfulfilled promise. Valla, Pico, Politian, and so many others, they all had died far too early, whereas in ancient times the scholars seemed to have attained a patriarchal old age. A lonely surviver, Erasmus was left to face old age and to long for his passing from this *tragicum seculum* into *alterum seculum,* the better future of eternity. [100] Some of his correspondents fully agreed with such a pessimistic view. [101] Erasmus himself was left occasional sparks of hope such as the progress of the *Collegium Trilingue* at Louvain and the flattering

---

[94] E.g. Allen 1.107 (June 1489?).

[95] Allen 1.273 (December 1499), 2.331 (August 1516), 2.485 (February 1517).

[96] Allen 1.163 (November 1496; Erasmus mentions no names, but that he was thinking of Italians may be inferred from the context of LB 1.1010B); Allen 2.99f. (May 1515).

[97] Allen 2.70.

[98] Allen 2.80.

[99] Allen 2.265, 487f., 492f., 3.384, 581, 588; in the famous letter to Capito Italian humanism is represented by two physicians only (Allen 2.489).

[100] Allen 5.243-8; cf. 6.149.

[101] Allen 6.123, 238f.

invitations of Francis I, but the emphasis now was nostalgic frustration: it needed so little to get things going in a very different way. [102]

And yet, not long afterwards, we find a changed Erasmus, hopefully watching out for the final fulfilment of his vision, though he no longer used the term 'Golden Age'. Spring and summer 1527 must indeed have been one of the happy periods in Erasmus' life. A fair number of important works left the presses, while his letters showed unusual vigour and originality. Complaints about his health were rare, and less energy was devoured by unconstructive polemics between February and August 1527 than in the previous and subsequent correspondence. With satisfaction Erasmus noted the death of some of his obstinate enemies, obviously a God-willed change for the better. [103]

The brightening-up was partly caused by new manifestations of high favour: in particular the letters to John III of Portugal and Sigismund I of Poland showed how much good, both for himself and for Christendom, Erasmus expected from these outsiders among the princes of Europe. [104] Stern admonitions from More and Tunstall had forced upon him the long due clarification of his position in the religious controversy. Erasmus' reply to More, [105] in April, stated his case with some famous formulations, and at the same time he began working on the second book of *Hyperaspistes* which largely juxtaposed Luther's positions with those of some early Christian heretics and attempted to confute both with the help of the orthodox fathers. [106] More than ever would the opinions of fathers now form a touchstone of a truly Christian mind. From the same period date some remarkable letters of dedication, prefacing the important editions of fathers published in these months. [107]

It can hardly come as a surprise that, during this period, Erasmus persistently viewed the future in a more hopeful mood. With new vigour and optimism he expressed his hope in Christ as the spiritual doctor and *deus ex machina*. [108] A letter to Warham in May repeated significantly the very factors which twelve years earlier had induced Erasmus to predict the coming of a Golden Age: the rage of his enemies is but dismay about the waning of their fame, while everywhere the language and *bonae litterae* blossom forth with happy success. Within a few years the scene of human affairs will be reversed and that moderation which Erasmus always showed in his writings will be embraced by all theologians. The princes themselves in their wisdom will have to restrain the antihumanists, lest troubles worse than the present Lutheran fire inflame the world. [109]

---

[102] Allen 5.562, 6.51f.
[103] Allen 7.53, 66.
[104] Allen 6.483ff., 7.59ff., cf. 105f., 148, 158f.
[105] Allen 7.5ff.
[106] LB 10.1337ff.; cf. Allen 7.116f.
[107] Cf. the prefaces to editions of Chrysostom (Allen 6.467ff., 483ff., 7.95ff., 126f.), Origen (Allen 7.101ff.), and Ambrose (Allen 7.118ff.).
[108] Allen 7.53, 61f., 68, and still 162, 164.
[109] Allen 7.75f.

Erasmus thus had gained a fresh and precious confidence that his efforts will not be thwarted and his ideals will succeed with the help of Christ. This new optimism animated him time and again in his remaining years, although the opposite feelings of despair and frustration were perhaps more frequent and, at any rate, more noted by posterity. Most remarkable perhaps was the revival of optimism in the winter of 1531-2, ushered in by circumstances strikingly similar to the situation of early 1527. Immediately upon the news of Zwingli's death Erasmus sat down and wrote rejoicingly to Amerbach: "my stomach happily has come to life again, and so far nature conducts herself so obligingly as regards my afflictions that I cannot wish for anything better. *Deest convictor lepidus, et animus curis vacuus.* [Erasmus mocking medieval rhymes!] True that Beda will not keep quiet, but as we are involved in this ruthless age, we must set our mind firmly to face everything". [110] A month later Amerbach informed Erasmus of the death of Oecolampadius. Erasmus reacted in a subtle, but unambiguous way when writing to Grynaeus, a friend of the dead reformer. "The death of Oecolampadius will affect men variously, each one according to his convictions. I pray that God pity him, for this is what we all need." [111] Three days later, however, when writing to Campeggio, Erasmus jubilantly commented on the death of the two "pillars of the sacramental sect", and added in conclusion: "...the Lord alone can cure these fatal evils, and he is resolved that the praise for it be given to him rather than to human schemes and actions." [112]

Of this particular period few letters by Erasmus exist, but they significantly reappraise the revival of true learning. If one or two months earlier some hope for future happiness had barely been hinted at, Erasmus now, in November, talked again of the *politiores disciplinae* which may be seen in this century happily blossoming forth in every nation". [113] Two young Polish students he deemed fortunate, "first of all because you are born in this century which admirably revived sincerity both in true piety and literary accomplishments." [114] On the same day he passed the news of the death of the two reformers to Mary of Hungary and expressed his hope that with God's assistance this lesson will cause a widespread change of opinion. In the same letter, written in the middle of December, Erasmus fancied the comforting allegory of winter and sadness that had taken to their heels, while the flowers of joy were budding. [115] In February 1532 Froben published his edition of Basil, and Erasmus contributed an epistle dedicatory which again reflected the enthusiasm of these months. [116]

---

[110] Allen 9.366 (24 October 1531).
[111] Allen 9.393 (29 November 1531).
[112] Allen 9.395f. (2 December 1531).
[113] Allen 9.381, cf. 373 and the desperate statements of 9.13, 257.
[114] Allen 9.401.
[115] Allen 9.400.
[116] Allen 9.435f. (to Sadoleto): Erasmus had firmly made up his mind to refuse any further requests for prefaces. "Sed ab hac adamantina, ut mihi quidem videbatur, sententia me transversum abripuit Divus Basilius, vir optimo iure dictus Magnus, sed

We have been discussing Erasmus' changing attitudes to his own day at some length; the following conclusions may justify this procedure. While the hope for a universal *pax Christiana* to be accomplished by the learning of the Christian humanists and the support of the secular princes remained, the term 'Golden Age' ceased to be associated with this hope after the second decade of the 16th century. Would Erasmus have dropped the term in his later days, because he no more approved of the strong political implications which he had formerly given to it? It is easy to see how his ideas differed genuinely from the common notion of progressive development in the secular sphere. What he emphasized in his later years is that a turn for the better will depend on God's favour and Christ's direct intervention.

VIII

What is the place of Erasmus' Golden Age of Christian humanism within the threefold pattern of the 'Renaissance' conception? As we shall now attempt to show, it never had its historical precedent in the classical Golden Age at the dawn of human history, to which Erasmus referred in the *Praise of Folly,* nor in that Golden Age of Christ and the Apostles, the fulfilment of the promise allegorically held out to the pagans, which he celebrated in *Antibarbari.* [117] The era of Christian humanism, in achievement, crisis, and hope, finds its true historical precedent in the age of the Christian fathers, for which Erasmus does not seem to have used the term 'Golden Age'.

Despite all the importance he may have attached to the classic period of Graeco-Roman antiquity or to the era of Christ and the Apostles, there can be no doubt that his heart as well as the greater part of his life-work spent in scholarship belonged to the fathers of the second, third, and fourth centuries. Never did Erasmus create a consistent picture of this age and rarely did he sketch any of its general features. What his biographies and prefaces to texts of Athanasius, Ambrose, Augustine, Basil, Chrysostom, Irenaeus, Jerome, Gregory, Origen, and still others bring to life is the personality of the individual father as it emerges from the comparison with

---

Maximi cognomine dignior. Ex his quae versa legeram, veluti per nebulam, suspiciebam ingenii dotes plane divinas, ac pectus humana conditione maius. Verum simulatque contigit audire Christianum Demosthenem, imo coelestem oratorem, sua lingua loquentem, sic animum meum totum perculit inflammavitque vere flexanima divinitus afflati Praesulis eloquentia ut mihi nihil prius curandum duxerim quam ut inaestimabilis hic thesaurus in publicam utilitatem typis evulgaretur. ... Haec est enim illa, cuius somnium modo vidit Plato, vere pulcherrima rerum sapientia, quae spiritualibus oculis conspecta incredibiles excitat amores sui....

[117] LB 4.433D, 10.1712C.

other individual fathers. [118]   If sometimes only for the sake of contrast, they are invariably viewed together.   Beyond the liberties of individual thought, they all express the crucial consensus of Christendom.

The names of several fathers often appear in company, as if Erasmus wished to identify a historical period to which he cannot otherwise put a name.   But more than a mode of expression, such a grouping of individuals was often his sole way of shaping his perception of history. [119]   Erasmus knew the political history of the third and fourth centuries surprisingly well, but to arrange the facts into a comprehensive narrative might rather have distorted the historical picture which he wanted to save from oblivion.   The common bonds which he clearly saw in the lives of the various fathers spelled out the essential problems and achievements of their age.   The fathers were almost, but not quite, superhuman, *athletae Dei,* [120] closer to God than to the average mankind, the closest earthly approximation to Christ and the Apostles who dissociated themselves from human history by the fulness of their divinity.   The very simplicity of manners of the apostolic age still persisted in the patristic one, [121] although in another respect the fathers, in the humanists' view, must surpass "the rustic and inexperienced... fishermen" of the New Testament: they of all Christians inherited the full benefit of the classical civilization.   Its education they imbibed, its language they continued, [122] often popularizing it to reach the urban masses of the hellenistic east, [123] exactly as their commentaries on the Scriptures interpreted the divine mysteries to the popular mind by launching the method of allegorical interpretation. [124]

But quiet striving for Christian scholarship alone did not give to the age of the fathers its peculiar flavour.   This age was crucial, not despite, but because of its inherent dangers.   The achievements of the fathers stood out against the background of a deadly crisis for young Christendom.   In so far as the dangers were merely political ones, they were not often allowed to enter Erasmus' biographical surveys; [125] what he observed with a sort of bewildered fascination were the many heresies, sprawling forth with vigour

---

[118] Allen 8.147, 9.268, 328, 436ff.: "...contumeliae genus est virum divinitus afflatum cum prophanis ac nihil aliud quam hominibus conferre. Decentius est divum cum divis componere"; LB 5.844CD.

[119] E.g. Allen 8.379: "...in canonicis scripturis ac priscis illis doctoribus, Cypriano, Hilario, Ambrosio, Hieronymo, Augustino, Basilio, Chrysostomo, quorum scripta plurimum adhuc referunt spiritus Apostolici, studiose versatus", and similarly: "...tales viros apparet ante Bonaventurae, Thomae, Scoti, Alberti Magni atque etiam Petri Lumbardi tempora floruisse."

[120] *Hieronymi vita* 575; Allen 4.27, 5. 467.

[121] Erasmus evidently distinguishes between an apostolic age and a patristic one when stating that Irenaeus still was *vicinus* to the time of the Apostles (Allen 6.385); Jerome, on the other hand, is said to have left Rome because the *Christiana simplicitas* was being corrupted there (*Hieronymi vita* 670f.).

[122] Allen 3.316ff., 5.101ff., 6.253, 390, 9.268, 436; LB 10.1736B.

[123] Allen 5.102.

[124] Allen 5.102f., 110, 6.486f.

[125] Allen 5.472, 7.122f.; LB 5.88AB.

and obstinacy and often backed by the power of the authorities. Erasmus' preface to patristic editions are saturated with references to, and sometimes proper lists of, the various heretical movements. [126] As the heresies originated from pagan philosophies, the classical eloquence of fathers featuring the Christian orthodoxy would represent the obvious remedy, for Erasmus respected, as it were, a rule of Renaissance medicine that nature from the same fold produced both the disease and its cure. [127] It was a breathtaking responsibility which the handful of sound Christian scholars had to cope with, for the larger numbers of brave martyrs and would-be martyrs had no intellectual contribution to make. [128]

The age of the fathers was, Erasmus felt, strikingly similar to his own time, with the humanists struggling for the revival of learning and Christian life, with the storm of heresies gathering momentum and the stupid monks continuing the useless role of the early martyrs.

The Christian humanists were, indeed, the true sons of the Christian fathers. In one of the earliest preserved letters Erasmus suggested to his friend Cornelius Gerard that their exchange of letters be conducted in the spirit of the correspondence between Jerome and Augustine. Still in 1531 he felt that the same two fathers shared exactly his own problems and misfortunes. [129] In another letter he viewed the Strasbourg civic commonwealth of his friends around Wimpheling as the possible realization of the Platonic state in the interpretation of Jerome. The key note in this text is *concordia*. It is the same *concordia,* rather than orthodox rigour, to which the fathers are devoted in their defense against heresies. [130] Heresies interested Erasmus immensely. In addition to the well-known juxtaposition of Luther with some early arch-heretics, he even recalled the pre-Christian and medieval heresies. In his commentary on Psalm 83 he inserted what might be termed a historical outline of the progress of heretical movements. [131]

---

[126] See e.g. Allen 5.105, where a clue for the dates of Arnobius' life is obtained from some heresies which he mentions and others which he could hardly have failed to mention in case he had known them.

[127] Consequently Origen may be studied as a truly Christian author, for the sound texture of his Christian scholarship by far outweighs the few ulcers of heresy, whereas Seneca for his own sake must be considered a heathen. As a pagan he must be praised for some general agreement with the tenets of Christianity; as a Christian he ought to be condemned for his disagreement with essential doctrines: Allen 4.508, 7.101ff., 8.29.

[128] LB 10.1724F-1725A: "In summa, frustra illi [the martyrs] pro Christi doctrina sanguinem fortiter fudissent, ni hi [the scholarly fathers] ab haereticis eam suis litteris vindicassent"; in fact, we are more indebted to some of the heretics than to the martyrs; cf., however, LB 5. 390CD, 1296D; Allen 6.385: these later statements sound differently.

[129] Allen 1.104; Augustine, *Epistolae* 166.1; Allen 9.233; cf. 3.337. When Erasmus dedicated to Archbishop Lasky the works of Ambrose, that great bishop and intrepid pastor, a Homeric verse came to his mind which he had, years ago, included in the *Adagia*: "thus the God joins always one like man to another": Allen 7.121; cf. LB 2.80B, 4.414B; Homer, *Odyssey* 17.218.

[130] Allen 2.19, 6.385.

[131] LB 5.474ff.; cf. 9.524B: "nec uila tamen aetas caruit suis haeresibus, nec unquam est caritura; LB 9.545E, 871E, 10.1314ff., 1594A, 1630Cff.; Allen 5.465.

Erasmus considered the age of the Christian fathers to be a crucial period because it offered both the model problems and remedies which would return in other historical ages, in particular his own day. A problem like heresy revealed to him an essential line of historical continuity. In the same way, the 'Church' of the Christians at heart before and after the coming of Christ and classical erudition, which contained in substance all conceivable civilization, [132] were such lines of continuity that would necessarily disrupt every determined attempt at historical periodization.

Therefore, Erasmus is neither an evader nor a renegade from the 'modern' idea of historical progress. He simply views human history as one plane. Ultimately it has no structural pattern and thus appears all the more complex. There is, however, a second, superior plane of history. There lies, like the sky above the valley of human history, the timeless, unhistorical continuity of *historia sacra*. As the *Commentary on Psalm 33* and the *adagium "Sileni Alcibiadis"* show, flashes of light from above may reveal in some men of the past the *figurae* of eternal history.

The essence of this approach to history is evident already from a work of Erasmus' youth. The argument of *Antibarbari* takes its departure from a crucial question in the 'Renaissance' conception of history: when and why did the lamentable and shameful decay of classical culture occur? The point which Erasmus wants to prove is that ancient culture was not doomed by the arrival of Christianity as such. Hence the literary refinements of pagan antiquity were neither then nor now incompatible with the truth revealed by the Son of Man and the rustic Apostles. The "Golden Age" of Christ's human life does indeed create an all-important *connexus* between the *bonae litterae* and the Christian religion, not so much, however, in the sense of a unique and momentary historical situation. That Christ "wanted that *aureum seculum,* into which he resolved to be born, to be served by all previous and subsequent ages" must be understood in the light of the *seculum Christianum* mentioned just after which was prepared by so many "figures and mysteries" of world history. Christ here is the Christ *exaltatus...a terra,* the human Christ exalted to heaven, who dwells in both planes of history and links them in his twofold nature. "For his republic Christ prearranged all the pagans' valiant deeds and wise words, ingenious thoughts and industrious traditions. ...Their age did not ripen this crop of accomplishments just for its own benefit, but for us". [133]

From the timeless height of Christ's republic we must look back on Erasmus' adherence to the 'Renaissance' pattern of history. He did perceive a temporal climax on either side of the Dark Ages, a climax that was manifest in the ideals of the Christian fathers and the Christian humanists respectively. On the other hand, he knew that history never quite repeats itself. But individuality, as Erasmus understood it, would not necessarily

---

[132] Cf. the epistle dedicatory to the first edition of *Adagia* (Allen 1.291): "Quid enim probabilius quam quod nemo non dicit? Quem tot aetatum, tot nationum consensus non permoveat?"; cf. Valla's famous preface to *Elegantiae* (*Opera,* ed. Garin, 1.4).
[133] LB 10.1712C-1713B.

conflict with a recurrent historical situation. The individual is but an actor and, while his acting may be original, the act he performs is, at best, a *figura* of eternal values. Historical ages too may mirror Christ's republic in various ways and degrees, and yet in the varying reflections there recurs the same ideal.

IX

What were the sources from which Erasmus developed his concept of history? On past pages we were repeatedly reminded of patristic models; in conclusion we must now assemble the evidence in support of our opinion that the outstanding contribution of Erasmus to the study of history lies in a revival of certain patristic ideas. An adaptation rather than an imitation, this revival would seem unprecedented insofar as it represents a concious and deliberate choice, a reaction to the contemporary boom in old and new secular approaches to history. It has been said that a most conspicuous divergence with regard to history presented the crucial issue in the contest between pagan classicism and the Christian fathers.[134] In turn, Erasmus' eager reappraisal of patristic concepts of history may well furnish a distinctive mark for his own type of humanism.

We have attempted to show that Erasmus kept aloof from the broad avenues which were opened up by Cicero's patriotic and rhetorical approach to history as well as by the systematically scientific and political one of the Greeks. Nor would Eusebius and the other chroniclers of the Church militant down to the Middle Ages seem to offer more than occasional parallels to Erasmus' approach to history. Typically, Erasmus would question the veracity of historians in almost identical terms, whether he is referring to Herodotus and Thucydides or to Eusebius and other historiographers of early Christianity.[135] Only *Acts,* as part of the Scriptural

---

[134] C.N. Cochrane, *Christianity and Classical Culture,* Oxford 1940, 456.

[135] Cf. the following statements with Erasmus' references to Greek and Roman historians as quoted above in n. 2:

LB 6.433E-434B (Commentary on *Acts* 1.1): "Apud me certe nulla est dubitatio, quin Spiritus Sanctus ad fidei nostrae certitudinem hoc opus [*Acta*] superesse voluerit, nec ultra tamen proferri rerum gestarum historiam.... Etenim si legas ea, quae caeteri qui feruntur fuisse vicini temporibus Apostolorum, litteris prodiderunt..., videberis tibi fabulas, ut ita dixerim, legere, si conferas cum gravitate fideque huius Historiae. ... Huius generis esse puto scripta Clementis et Papiae, fortassis et Dionysii. ... Homines erant, et humanibus affectibus obnoxii. Quod si statim in his qui vixerant cum Apostolis reperta est suspicio vel erroris, vel vanitatis, quid futurum arbitraris fuisse, si talium narrationum aut scriptorum auctoritas longo successionis ordine transisset ad posteros? Summa cura parique fide contexuit Ecclesiasticam historiam Eusebius Caesariensis. At quam multa illic referuntur, quae nihil habent gravitatis ecclesiasticae?"

LB 9.472AB: Beda had taken exception at the following statement in Erasmus' epistle dedicatory to his paraphrase on *Corinthians* (Allen 3.480ff.): "De nascentis

canon, presents the integral truth of history endorsed by the Holy Spirit and thus superior to human critique. Since truth stems from revelation rather than historical investigation, those whom Erasmus associates with the Bible in the discovery of essential truth are not the historians, whether pagan or Christian, but the moral philosophers of classical antiquity, the Jewish prophets, and the Christian fathers.

Like the fathers at the dawn of the Christian era, Erasmus faces a choice between the Bible and profane history. He accepts the Scriptures as the central revelation of what happens in history and as a source that cannot be understood without the technique of allegorical interpretation. While both this principle and this technique had been in constant use throughout the Middle Ages, one might emphasize, as Cassirer has done with regard to Ficino's allegorizing mysticism, [136] that Erasmus accepts them in a 'relaxed', adogmatic form. Among many possible interpretations, the human mind is free to choose in the light of its own rational capacity. The first part of Erasmus' *Commentary on Psalm 33* must once more be adduced here. While borrowing most of its topics from patristic sources, it nevertheless supplies some lucid examples of philological and common sense criticism of patristic allegorization and ends on a very personal note with a long quotation from the Sermon of the Mount and the avowal of that *doctrina Christi* which is so different from *sapientia mundi* and must be gained from simple obedience to Christ's commands. [137] The modern reader will readily admit the acumen of Erasmus' criticisms of patristic allegorizing, but he will probably be less impressed with the second part of the treatise where Erasmus abandons the general guidance provided by Augustine's and Basil's commentaries on the same Psalm and gives a somewhat unexciting verse to verse interpretation of his own.

Like historical truth, Erasmus approaches historical time with the criteria of early Christianity. Unconcerned with the concept of time in the abstract he ignores the Greek metaphysical view of circular *chronos* in favour of the spontaneous experience of particular *kairoi*. Erasmus is constantly aware of those *kairoi* which had become crucial to early Christianity: Christ's redemption and Christ's *parousia* on the last day. But *kairoi* he also recognizes in the actions of Christ-like men in all times; suffice it to recall his succession of *Sileni*. Like the chain of prophets in the Old Testament, Erasmus' consecutive *kairoi* form the vital points of contact between the development of human history and the changeless continuity of *historia*

Ecclesiae primordiis ... prope nihil esse proditum historia graviore cuique tuto possis credere." In his *Responsio* to Beda Erasmus defends the statement: "Actorum Apostolicorum historiam excipio in eo ipso loco. Praeterea si qua est historia cui per omnia tuto licet credere, eam lubens videro, si quis commonstret. Etenim in ipsius Eusebii Ecclesiastica, et Tripartita quam vocant historia, multa sunt quae non possis tuto credere."

[136] E. Cassirer, Ficino's Place in Intellectual History, *Journal of the History of Ideas* 6 (1945), 494ff.

[137] LB 5.383BC.

sacra. Though even the dogmas of the Church were subject to change,[138] the Word itself was everlasting. When Erasmus paraphrases *Hebrews* 13.8: "Jesus is the same yesterday, today and into the ages", he adds: *"ita semper manebit illius doctrina"*.[139]

Up to this point, Erasmus' approach to time need not be linked to any particular strand within the patristic tradition; but if some further elements are taken into consideration, it is difficult not to be reminded of his great familiarity with the works of Origen and, through Origen, with the thought of the Alexandrian school. Among the gnostic heritage of Clement and Origen, O. Cullmann lists the "rejection of the Primitive Christian eschatological expectation, whose characteristic distinction in terms of time between the present and the future age is replaced by the Greek metaphysical distinction between this world and the timeless Beyond".[140] Many references, in particular those to the theatre of history, show that to Erasmus eternity differs from temporality by degrees of reality and is, at any rate, no simple continuation in time. The distinction between the stage of profane history and the reality of *historia sacra* is spatial rather than temporal: in the *kairos* of the play's *catastrophe* the *deus ex machina* touches down upon the stage, as it were, from the sphere of truth above.

In *Contra Celsum* both Celsus and Origen call Christ the leader of the chorus, (*chorostates*),[141] thus anticipating an image that Erasmus was to use frequently. The appearance of drama in the first lines of Erasmus' *Commentary on Psalm 33* is directly inspired by Origen's commentary on *Romans,*[142] a text that, as we shall see, was crucial to Erasmus. One may also be reminded of the opening passage of Origen's famous exposition of the Song of Songs,[143] whereas in contrast there is no similar reference in Augustine's commentary on Psalm 33, otherwise often closely followed in Erasmus' text.

The most daring consequence of the association of history with the stage, Erasmus' identification of Christ with the classical *deus ex machina*,

---

[138] LB 10.1546C; cf. above p. 31.

[139] LB 7.1196E.

[140] O. Cullmann, *Christ and Time,* transl. F.V. Filson, London 1951, 56.

[141] Origen, *Contra Celsum* 5.33.

[142] Cf. the passage in Erasmus' *Commentary* quoted above in n. 3 with *Romans* 11.8: "Sicut scriptum est: Dedit illis Deus spiritum compuctionis: oculos ut non videant, et aures ut non audiant, usque in hodiernum diem", and with Origen's commentary on *Romans* 11.8 (Migne, P.G. 14.1181): "Vide ergo si hoc modo possumus explicare quod quaeritur. Sicut oculis corporeis utitur unusquisque ad videndum sive bona, sive mala, et in potestate habet elevare oculos ad coelum, et per id quod videt, conditorem eius agnoscere, et collaudare creatorem, vel conferre ad spectacula circi, vel theatri, vel quarumlibet sordidarum oblectamenta visionum, quibus aut ad libidinem, aut ad rapacitatem, vel alia quaeque vitia animus inflammetur: ita mihi intelligi etiam animae oculos..." In his own paraphrase to *Romans* 11.8 Erasmus emphasizes the continuous succession of the blind and deaf unbelievers: "Tales olim erant Prophetis, tales fuerunt ipsi Christo, tales et in hunc usque diem sunt Evangelii praeconibus" (LB 7.813E).

[143] Origen, *Commentarium in Cantica Canticorum,* Prologus.

would have been most unacceptable to Augustine, [144] but could be understood in the light of Origen's *"mysterion"* of Christ's symbolic presence in the Church where "the historic life of the historical Christ and the historic life of the mystical Christ...are but one...". [145]

While in the title of Psalm 33 both Augustine and Erasmus identify *David* with Christ and *Abimelech* with unspiritual man who fails to receive Christ, Erasmus mostly thinks of the *logos* and cautiously evades Augustine's concrete identifications with the Eucharist and the Son of Man who was crucified by the Jews. [146] Already the christology of Clement failed to satisfy modern theologians, [147] and not by chance, if perhaps exaggeratedly, have both Origen and Erasmus been accused of sacrificing the historical Christ to the philosophical *logos*. Allegedly they both undervalue the dogma of the incarnation. [148] Both were indeed preoccupied with the expectation of Christ's final *parousia*. If this could lessen their consideration for Christ's redeeming death on the cross, the same would also result from their emphatic assertion of human Free Will. We have tried to show that in Erasmus' view the *kairos* of the Son incarnate does not present a unique mid-point of history; at least Erasmus never acknowledged its significance in terms of history comparable to the crucial role which that historical moment plays in Augustine's *City of God* or still in Dante's *Monarchy*.

Although allegorization of the Old Testament is, of course, common practice, Erasmus' use of it in the *Commentary on Psalm 33* is certainly apt to recall the conclusions of Cullmann who indicts gnosticism of "rejection of the Old Testament, both in its explanation of history as the creative action of God and in its claim that the history of Israel constitutes redemptive history". [149] It is true that Erasmus starts out on his commentary with the indication that *"historia contextitur libro Regnorum primo, capite XXI"*. But in recounting at some length the historical background against which the Psalm was composed by David and against which it must be interpreted, he had not the slightest intention of writing redemptive history. The historical sketch is of the substance of the "husk" and not the "barley". It is no more than the routine exercise of that methodical text criticism in view of which A. Harnack has, again, brought together the names of Erasmus and Origen. [150]

---

[144] See C.N. Cochrane, *Christianity and Classical Culture* 479.

[145] H. von Balthasar, Le Mystérion d'Origène, *Recherches de science religieuse* 27 (1936), 544; cf. 558f.

[146] LB 5.380-383; cf. in particular 381B-382F with Augustine, *Enarratio in Ps. 33,* 2.2
        391A-C   "   "   "   2.7.

[147] C. Bigg, *The Christian Platonists of Alexandria* 103.

[148] R.C.P. Hanson, *Allegory and Event* 276-283; A. Harnack, *History of Dogma,* 2London 1897ff., 3.270; H.A.E. van Gelder, *The Two Reformations of the 16th Century,* The Hague 1961, 140ff.

[149] O. Cullmann, *Christ and Time* 55.

[150] A. Harnack, *History of Dogma* 6.173: "...the Humanist Erasmus not only laid the foundation of textual criticism of the New Testament and scientific patrology, but carried them at once to a high state of perfection. From a taste for the original, criticism grew up. What dies out in the Church with Origen, nay, in some measure

In fact, it is surprising that Erasmus should have chosen to make this Psalm the receptacle of his thoughts about history. In commenting on Psalm 33, he accepts willingly, but not uncritically, some inspiration both from the pastoral and edifying commentary on the same text by Basil the Great [151] and from the allegorizing one by Augustine. [152] Neither father, however, spoke of history. In a sense, the very difference between the two patristic commentaries may have prompted Erasmus to think more deeply about the Biblical *historia* and its conduciveness to truth. If this were so, his thought might almost naturally have turned to Origen. The fact that the introductory contrast between the true, edifying spectacles and the false, injurious ones is gleaned from Origen sufficiently proves that the Alexandrine father was uppermost in Erasmus' mind when he set out to formulate his judgment on history. We know by now that it was Erasmus' constant tendency to dismantle history of its solid facts, to understand it merely as a parable; this indeed would seem to be the legacy of the persistent Alexandrine approach to "history in terms of prophecy and fulfilment". [153] Essentially it was Origen who introduced in Christian exegesis the method of figurative interpretation by which one character or event is understood as the *figura* of another, subsequent character or event. With Origen Erasmus maintains that the Old Testament in certain statements is deliberately absurd so that the thoughtful reader might be compelled to realize the presence of a mystery. "The letter kills..."; Erasmus repeats Paul's words quite unequivocally, but adds that they do not always apply. [154]

"I can learn more Christian philosophy from one page by Origen than from ten by Augustine". The famous words, written to Eck in 1518, [155] are meant very seriously. They show Erasmus facing what was, in a sense, the cross-roads of his life. His choice, no less formidable than that of Hercules, ultimately also accounts for his attitude towards history. Erasmus' faith in Origen and his suspiciousness of Augustine, both hinge around the problem of Free Will.

---

even before Origen, or what—keeping out of view a few Antiochians—had never really developed themselves strongly, namely, historic sense and historic exegesis, developed themselves now." On the other hand, cf. 2.343 about Origen: "In the final utterances of religious metaphysics ecclesiastical Christianity, with the exception of a few compromises, is thrown off as a husk. The objects of religious knowledge have no history or rather, and this is a genuinely Gnostic and Neoplatonic idea, they have only a supramundane one."

[151] E.g. LB 5.379BC: Basil, *Homil. in Psalmos* 16.1
      388AB: 16.1 (end)
      389EF: 16.2 (beginning)
      383BC: 16.5

[152] Cf. LB 5. 376D-F, 378E, 381BC, 382EF, 391AB with Augustine, *Enarratio in Ps. 33*, 1.9-11, 2.2, 2.7.

[153] R.L.P. Milburn, *Early Christian Interpretations of History*, London 1954, 23 et passim.

[154] LB 5.373DE, 870B; cf. R.L.P. Milburn, *Early Christian Interpretations of History* 38ff.; R.C.P. Hanson, *Allegory and Event* 239ff.

[155] Allen 3.337.

Though Augustine often asserted man's freedom, it is for him "reduced to the choice between one and another sin", ...while he "insists again and again on the completely gratuitous character of God's gift of salvation to the few". [156]   In contrast, the Alexandrines maintain for Christians and pagans alike the freedom to do good or evil and thus to cooperate with Christ's work of salvation. [157]   Typically, Origen's painstaking commentary on *Romans* becomes Erasmus' steady source of inspiration when, in his own annotations to Paul's epistle and later in his paraphrase of it, he faces up to Paul's powerful emphasis on the gratuitous character of salvation.   Again as commentator of *Romans,* Origen becomes Erasmus' key witness against Luther. [158]

Although history was not directly an issue when both Eck and Luther criticized Erasmus for his lack of enthusiasm for Augustine, it must here be noted that Augustine's confident reliance on systematic exploration and interpretation of history correspond directly with his reserved attitude towards Free Will.   In his approach to history Augustine rejects what C.N. Cochrane has called: "the humanist compromise, the notion that man shares with 'circumstance' the determination of his destiny". [159]   This humanist compromise is called into operation not only when Thucydides and Polybius, or later Machiavelli, recognize in history a clash between human will and the classical concept of fortune, but also when the Alexandrines, and later Erasmus, balance against that same human will the Christian concept of predestination.   Augustine had set the example, and Christian historiography would forever continue to find in historical patterns and laws the expression of God's omniscience and omnipotence.   Consequently, Erasmus must instinctively have opposed such patterns and laws of history as they seemed to limit the free exercise of human responsibility.   And, again, such laws are conspicuously absent from the thought of Origen.

---

[156] H.A. Deane, *The Political and Social Ideas of St. Augustine,* New York 1963, 19; cf. 25ff.   Erasmus states his point as follows: "Divus Augustinus adversus Pelagium toto studio dimicans, alicubi minus tribuit Libero Arbitrio quam tribuendum putant qui nunc in scholis regnant theologicis" (Allen 5.183); and: "quod si sequar Paulum et Augustinum perpusillum est quod relinquitur Libero Arbitrio" (Allen 7.8).

[157] C. Bigg, *The Christian Platonists of Alexandria* 110f.: "...Augustine did not hesitate to maintain that, though God predestines, He is yet not the author of evil. But to the Alexandrines this did not seem possible. ... Hence they were driven to make Will an independent faculty, knowing both good and evil and choosing between them, selecting and in fact creating its own motive.   The actual phrase Free Will, *Liberum Arbitrium* is due to Tertullian [cf. editor's n.], but it expresses with Latin precision what Clement and Origen really mean."

[158] Already the *Argumentum in epistolam ... ad Romanos* (LB 6.547ff./7.774ff.) follows Origen very closely; cf. Erasmus' text with the introduction to Origen's commentary on *Romans.*   The parable which Erasmus introduces in his last paragraph is taken from Origen, *In Rom.* 5.1 (P.G. 14. 1007f.; cf. LB 10.1543A-C; cf. D.P. Walker, Origène en France au début du XVIᵉ siècle, *Courants religieux et humanisme,* Bibl. des centres d'études supérieures spécialisés, Paris 1959, 113ff.; E. Wind, The Revival of Origen, *Studies in Art and Literature for Belle da Costa Greene,* ed. D. Miner, Princeton U.P. 1954, 412-424; L. Febvre, *Origène et Des Périers,* Paris 1942; L. Giusso, *Origene e il Rinascimento,* Rome 1957.

[159] C.N. Cochrane, *Christianity and Classical Culture* 478.

From man's freedom of action stems the complexity of his nature that renders formidable the task of any prospective biographer. The *Hieronymi vita* is Erasmus' only full-fledged biography and, at that, his only substantial piece of systematic historical narrative. Typically, it owns its existence to a duty of love and not a desire to write history. Rather Erasmus feels he must vindicate the venerated father from the imputations of such professional historians as Rufinus. [160]

As Augustine saw human history, the *civitas terrena* was physically intermixed with the *civitas Dei* but respected its own, independent set of values. Poor as these values might be, they, nevertheless, became discernible principles of persistent world-historical development. [160] Augustine passionately rejected the cyclic theory of Stoicism and what relics thereof he discovered in Origen, but he affirmed and elaborated upon the pattern of six world ages according to the six days of Creation. [162] For appalling as the moral principles of the world might be, its historical development emanated from God and was leading again toward God. As the stage and witness of God's revelation and God's salvation, mundane history deserved the fullest attention. In the final analysis, mundane history was redemptive history; it had its crucial mid-point in the *kairos* of Christ's human existence, whereas pagan Greece and Rome, in Augustine's view, were basically anticlimactic to the age of Christ and the Apostles. Again and again we have noted that Erasmus tended to neglect or even oppose these basic assumptions of Augustine's view of history.

Erasmus too believed that the world was constituted upon its own, specific nature, but, in the final analysis, it was no more than the continuous negation of the spirit. [163] What really mattered was not the development of world history, but the flashlike illumination of world history by consecutive men of the spirit. Again we are faced with the historical concept that passes from Erasmus' *Sileni* to the spiritualist Sebastian Franck. Franck's tireless denunciations of the "*mundus*" and his avowal of holy heretics, [164] in turn, forecast the pietism of a Gottfried Arnold.

Augustine recognized brutal self-interest as the guiding principle of the *civitas terrena*. Erasmus' *adagium* "*Scarabeus aquilam quaerit*" proves sufficiently that he thought no better about this point. Nonetheless he expected of the secular princes that earthly peace which would inaugurate the Golden Age of Christian humanism. Unlike Augustine, Erasmus never succeeded in harmonizing the conflicting notions of political power deeply

---

[160] Most other biographical introductions to Erasmus' patristic editions stem from philological routine and supply the details relevant to text criticism; see below p. 95f.

[161] Augustine, *De civit. Dei* 15.4, 18.1-2, 5.12; cf. C.N. Cochrane, *Christianity and Classical Culture* 488ff.

[162] Augustine, *De civit. Dei* 11.5-7, 12.13-14; cf. Origen, *De principiis* 3.5.3; *Contra Celsum* 4.12-13.

[163] E.g. LB 5.206EF: "...Habet et hic mundus christos suos, reges et sacerdotes, quorum nonnulli cutem habent unctam, sed mentem inunctam. ... Habet Deus unctos suos, quos non vult laedi ab iis, quos unxit mundus. ..."; cf. LB 5. 483B-D, 607B.

[164] See below p. 50.

rooted in evil which, nevertheless, exercised justifiable coercion and established the salutary *pax terrena.* Instead he would again seem to follow the lead of Origen over against Augustine, Eusebius, and the Middle Ages when he increasingly refused to associate the *pax Romana* with the *pax Messianica,* [165] that is, in Erasmus' diction, the Golden Age under princely patronage with Christ's conclusive intervention in the historical drama.

The admiration for Origen and the intimate knowledge of some of his works, however, should not merely be linked to Erasmus' reserved attitude towards systematic history and historical analysis. The same Origen could demonstrate impressively that the command of historical facts, no less than the philological and literary command of words, was essential both for the profound penetration and the learned defense of Christ's true teaching. [166] *Cognitio rerum ac verborum*: perhaps no author was better equipped than Origen to direct the enlivening flow of Greek *paideia* towards Erasmus' *philosophia Christi.* Eager to acknowledge this debt, Erasmus not only praised Origen as the master of allegorical exegesis, [167] but also emphasized his unequalled zeal for *historia* in the sense of literal and philological interpretation. "*Cum nemo diligentius se gesserit in historia...*"; [168] in a general sense too the statement is perhaps true of Erasmus himself no less than of Origen, if we are willing to view them against the background of the apocalyptic days through which each of them lived.

X

In conclusion we must try to recall from preceding pages what would seem to us Erasmus' crucial thoughts of history. Moreover, we may yet come a step closer to the understanding of their significance, if we relate them to some other currents of historical thought in the 16th century. What Erasmus emphasized time and again may perhaps be summed up as follows.

---

[165] Cf. J. Daniélou, *The Lord of History*, transl. N. Abercombie, London 1958, 56; for Erasmus' dislike of Augustine's defense of just war: LB 6.242D, 319F and generally R.P. Adams, *The Better Part of Valor*, Seattle 1962; on Augustine's rejection of the pacifism and antimilitarism of Tertullian, Origen, and others: H.A. Deane, *The Political and Social Ideas of St. Augustine* 155ff.

[166] When reading *Contra Celsum* one is of course mostly impressed with Origen's solid knowledge of the Greek philosophers, but he also quotes Herodotus frequently and Josephus and Thucydides occasionally (cf. the indices of H. Chadwick's ed. in English translation, Cambridge 1953). For Origen's knowledge of facts and sense of history see e.g. *Contra Celsum* 1.42-47 (on historicity) and 1.14-16 (wisdom and antiquity of the Jews).

[167] LB 5.29D-F, 127D.

[168] LB 9.97A.

First; in view of the perfect truth of sacred history inspired by the Holy Spirit, all human records are necessarily unreliable. Divine intervention in history is perfectly real. Its reality must be contrasted with the figurative character of the play performed by human actors, who normally occupy the stage of history.

Second; even though a progress, or at least development, of specific institutions may be noted, such change is devaluated by the permanent and superior significance of basic immutables. The confidence in a continued, salutary progress of Christian scholarship, however, is increasingly overshadowed by the near-eschatological visions of a final crisis. Thus, various notions of development and continuity neutralize each other in the sensitive mind of Erasmus.

Third; the sense of history and historical knowledge prove themselves valuable tools in the methodical practice of critical philology; but philology alone does not justify the systematic occupation with history. Philology brings to light such truth as every text contains, whereas history, in its necessary biased account of facts, adds new errors to old ones.

Just how alone Erasmus stood in his views may be realized if one recalls that his *Commentary on Psalm 33* was published in the same year as Vives' *De disciplinis*. Melanchthon was then preparing and prefacing the first edition of Carion's *Chronicon*. Neither Vives nor Melanchthon can be accused of an uncritical attitude towards history and both were, like Erasmus, intimately acquainted with patristic literature. Yet, however much they differed among themselves in other respects, their first look at history was determined by an identical point of view. Both were teachers, whereas Erasmus was not. He did not ignore that the classics of historiography had an obvious and prominent place in education, but at the bottom of his heart he was a scholar and indifferent to educational practice. The problem of history which he faced could not be reduced to the educator's choice between the relative merits of various authors and methods.

Of course, Melanchthon did not reduce the value of history to its contribution in the field of education. Like Luther, he valued history because he confined in God as the maker and sole moderator of history. In this sense, all history was for both sacred history. [169] Only in the Scriptures was it recorded without error, but the Word of God supplied reliable criteria for the right understanding of secular history as well. It was edifying to encounter in any period of secular history the friends and foes of God, and it was a goodly lesson to realize that the foes had always outnumbered the

---

[169] P. Fraenkel, (*Testimonia Patrum*, Geneva 1961, 61, cf. 249) concludes "that Melanchthon knew only one kind of history and that was essentially sacred history". H. Zahrnt (*Luther deutet Geschichte*, Munich 1952, 18, 21) reaches the same conclusion for Luther and quotes: "Die Historien sind nichts anderes denn Anzeigung, Gedächtnis und Merkmal göttlicher Werk und Urteil". They show God, "wie er die Welt, sonderlich die Menschen, erhält, regiert, hindert, fördert, strafet und ehret", how he "hänget, rädert, enthäupt, würget und krieget". See also J.M. Headley, *Luther's View of Church History*, Yale U.P. 1963, 1ff., 53ff.

friends. It was this spirit that rendered possible the impressive mastering of world history achieved in the tradition stemming from Melanchthon. For it was essentially Melanchthon's concept of universal history that was taken over by his successors at the price of gradual secularization. [170]

Erasmus' approach would seem to differ from that of the Wittenbergers in emphasis rather than in kind, but here it is emphasis that counts. Luther saw in history "God's mummery" [171] and Melanchthon called it a "*proscenium Dei*". [172] Erasmus too would speak of the divine *choragus,* but normally the stage of history is occupied by human actors. It is men who act in history until the *deus ex machina* will descend in the hour of his *kairos.* This may point to divine aloofness and smack of gnosticism just as the emphasis on God's immanence in history serves to associate the Wittenbergers with Augustine.

But inference, for this is what has led to such accusations against Erasmus, could also be used in a different way. One could argue that Eramus was unwilling to celebrate, with Melanchthon, in secular history "the conservation of the world of nations under the secular arm of God", [173] because the historical records were so utterly unreliable. Melanchthon, as all confessional historians, was confident that with God's help, he could discover the true meaning of fallacious history. Erasmus, the sober philologist, must have deeply resented such assurance. Did he not resent it just as much when Luther set out to furnish with the help of God his own, peculiar interpretation of the Bible ?

It is only logical that in the dispute over Free Will, Luther defended the hidden *Ecclesia paucorum,* whereas Erasmus, the historian of the *Sileni,* emphasized the overwhelming consensus in front of which his opponent stood quite alone, as he thought. Erasmus did not oppose the historical concept of the *Ecclesia paucorum* as such which was closely comparable to his own *Sileni,* but he rejected the conclusions which Luther derived from this concept. The few scattered *Sileni* belonged to the lowly plane of human history where they would set a shining example amid the general corruption. God's truth, however, could only be established on the plane of supramundane history. From there it was confirmed, not by the odd *Silenus,* but by the solid consensus of the Holy fathers. [174] Only in addition to the patristic consensus

---

[170] A. Klempt, *Die Säkularisierung der universalhistorischen Auffassung,* Göttingen 1960, especially 20f., 27ff., 34ff.

[171] The course of the universe is "Gottes Mummerei, darunter er sich verbirgt und in der Welt so wunderlich regiert und rumort" (quoted by H. Zahrnt, *Luther deutet Geschichte* 21). Yet the same Luther took strong exception at a passage wherein Erasmus explained redemptive history in the terminology of the Greek drama: R. Padberg, *Erasmus als Katechet,* Freiburg i.B. 1956, 73.

[172] "Nec putate ea tantum exempla divinitus nobis monstrata esse, quae in Sacris Litteris perscripta sunt: totus hic mundus velut proscenium est Dei, in quo omnium officiorum exempla quotidie exhibet" (quoted by A. Klempt, *Säkularisierung* 22).

[173] Ibid. 27.

[174] LB 9.1219DE: "Sed donemus, sicuti re vera donandum est, fieri posse ut unicuipiam humili et idiotae revelet Spiritus, quod multis eruditis non revelavit, quandoquidem hoc nomine Christus gratias agit Patri, quod quae celasset sapientes et pru-

historical insight could render valuable ancillary services in the critical reconstruction of Christ's true teachings. In contrast, there was no consensus about secular history, and there was nothing to establish its truth.

Whereas the confessional spirit promoted a new interest in universal history, historical methodology, on the other hand, may have partly owed its growing popularity to the blinders which confessional censorship imposed upon historical narrative. Historians who chose methodology to avoid commitment and exposure would likely be indifferent to Erasmus' reappraisal of patristic views. Such fear of confessional bias, however, cannot yet have motivated Vives' preference for historical theory. With him one is reminded of the educational needs at a time when historical reading matter had become plentiful. The classical treatises on history had tendered advice to the potential historiographer, but now a new approach was needed to assist the student of history in his complicated task.

In *De disciplinis* Vives presented his considered recommendation and evaluating bibliography of history only after surveying various sources of historical error. [175] But even the discussion of untruth in history was unlike anything Erasmus ever wrote. For Vives it was an academic question and, at best, a philosophical one fashioned after Cicero and Lucian. Patrizi would later on allow himself to be genuinely embarrassed by the question whether history could ever be truthful. But for Patrizi, as in some measure for Vives, there existed a natural and convenient way out of this dilemma. He conceded that historians might cheat and err in so many details, but insisted that this did not rule out their general usefulness. [176] Whether or not it was clearly spelled out, the idea was legitimate that history could contain errors and still be instructive. One only had to recognize the errors, and Bodin, for one, laid down new criteria for a more sophisticated diagnosis. History, as it then seemed, was to be a regular science with its own terms of reference and basic techniques. It actually was not. Although the thoughts of Erasmus could hardly appeal to these skilful masters of history, they too were beset by the bewildering idea that they watched a play on the stage and no more. [177] When all was said, formidable Clio was as untamed as ever, eliciting a human experience beyond rational controls.

Outsiders rather than the well known historical circles of the 16th century may perhaps attest to the influence of Erasmus. One may have to

---

dentes, hoc est, scribas, pharisaeos et philosophos, revelasset νηπίοις, hoc est, simplicibus et iuxta mundum stultis. Et fortasse talis stultus fuit Dominicus, talis Franciscus, si licuisset illis suum sequi spiritum. Sed si Paulus suo seculo, quo vigebat donum hoc Spiritus, iubet probari spiritus, an ex Deo sint, quid oportet fieri hoc seculo carnali? Unde igitur explorabimus spiritus? Ex eruditione? Utrinque rabini sunt. Ex vita? Utrinque peccatores. In altera totus sanctorum chorus, qui statuunt Liberum Arbitrium...."

[175] See above n. 19.

[176] F. Patrizi, *Della Historia diece dialoghi,* Venice 1560, 24ff. The outcome of the argument is clouded by the fact that Patrizi, who defended the position here outlined, seems to admit defeat at the end of the dialogue.

[177] See above n. 77f.

wait for Montaigne to find an enthusiastic reader of historical works, and yet thoroughly unimpressed with the objective values of history. One will not expect in Montaigne the religious motivation of Erasmus' doubts about historical truth, but all the more he stressed another motive already found in Erasmus. What made him doubtful about history was his acute sense for the complexity of human nature. From absorbing self-observation Montaigne knew that historians and biographers must forever be eluded by the object of their inquiry. He knew that the judgment on persons and events must depend upon the circumstantial viewpoint of the observer, for *"toutes les contrarietez s'y treuvent selon quelque tour et en quelque façon"*. [178]

More directly, though perhaps with less sophistication, Sebastian Franck inherited Erasmus' reluctance to pass judgment on the men of past and present. This attitude accounted for the preservation of Erasmus' *Sileni* in the holy heretics of Franck's *Ketzerchronik*. Whereas many protestant historiographers were scrutinizing the past for the rare protestant *avant la lettre* and canonized some that the medieval Church had execrated, both Erasmus' *Sileni* and some of Franck's heretics had a fluctuating quality not normally found in the radical transvaluation typical of protestant historiography. They were not merely secret saints wickedly decried as heretics by those who, under the cloak of righteousness, were really the culprits; their nature was more ambiguous than that. Socrates, the prototype of Erasmus' *Sileni,* was in fact hideous, vulgar, and probably also immoral. Quite objectively he was all that and was still Socrates. Franck's holy heretics were intermingled with ordinary ones of whom nothing good was to be said. Ostensibly he measured them all with the same yardstick, only to demonstrate, however, that the superficially objective criteria of heresy were crushed under the weight of true holiness. Now this, if anything, would appear to be the essence of Erasmus' thoughts of history; its attempted objectivity cannot withstand the weight of truth.

---

[178] Montaigne, *Essais* 2.1; cf. 1.20 (end), 2.10 and 1.25: ...the student "practiquera, par le moyen des histoires, ces grandes ames des meilleurs siecles. C'est un vain estude, qui veult; mais qui veult aussi, c'est un estude de fruict inestimable.... Qu'il [le gouverneur] ne luy apprenne pas tant les histoires qu'à en iuger. C'est à mon gré, entre toutes, la matiere à laquelle nos esprits s'appliquent de plus diverse mesure: i'ay leu en Tite Live cent choses que tel n'y a pas leu; Plutarque y en a leu cent, oultre ce que i'y ay sceu lire, et à l'adventure oultre ce que l'aucteur y avoit mis..."

BIOGRAPHY AND PRESENTATION
OF CHARACTER IN THE WORK OF ERAMUS

I

In historical writing the term 'biography' denotes an attempt to evaluate the significance of an individual figure of the past. The study of biography would seem particularly suited, then, to shed some light on historical thought in the Renaissance period, as this period has long been noted for its thorough appreciation of individuality. The work of Erasmus may well be chosen as a starting point for such a study: he was no doubt one of the most complex individuals of his age and, while he wrote scarcely a page of historical narrative in the style of the chronicle, he devoted numerous passages to biography. The purpose of this essay is to survey this part of his work and to determine his approach to biography against the background of his views on history. To this end, we will consider Erasmus' use of biographical *exempla* in the rhetorical tradition, his casual observations about historical personalities, and his more comprehensive biographical portraits. It is hoped that the evidence thus assembled will be found sufficiently conclusive so as to justify our disregard of the autobiographical strand in Erasmus' work. The autobiographical material would undoubtedly be relevant to the problems we wish to consider, but its study involves some touchy controversies over crucial sources. As a result, the inclusion of autobiographical evidence would unduly prolong and complicate our discussion. A better understanding of Erasmus' use of biography and his views on individuality, we hope, will help to clarity his own place in history as well as the attitudes of his contemporaries.

Following a tradition that led back to Goethe and Voltaire, Jacob Burckhardt considered individualism as the logical explanation for the great interest freshly focused upon biography. In some famous pages of his *Civilization of the Renaissance in Italy* he outlined the role of biography and autobiography in that "Discovery of World and Man" which marked for him the transition from the Middle Ages to the modern era.[1] Burckhardt's

---

[1] J. Burckhardt, *The Civilization of the Renaissance in Italy,* transl. S.C.G. Middlemore, London 1944 (Phaidon Press), 199ff.

masterfully—or, as some thought, mystifyingly—restrained formulations have always tempted his many readers to draw far-reaching conclusions from which he himself had wisely abstained. All subsequent discussions of Renaissance biography hinged around his views. This is particularly true of two problems which must be borne in mind as we approach the biographical strand in the work of Erasmus: the relationship of history and biography, and the emergence of individuality. Since there are as yet no adequate and comprehensive answers to these problems and since we must not set out from preconceived opinions if the evidence contained in Erasmus' work is to assist us in elucidating the thought of his contemporaries, we must approach the questions as they evolved.

According to Burckhardt, Italians of the Renaissance excelled in "the development of the individual", whence they acquired "remarkable power and inclination accurately to describe man as shown in history, according to his inward and outward characteristics". In developing Burckhardt's views one could say that with the private letters which Petrarch addressed to Cicero and other luminaries of classical antiquity an exciting dialogue with the greatest spirits of the past had begun. Saturated with an intimate appreciation of individuality, this dialogue added completely new dimensions to historical insight. It presented the figures of the past as children of time and circumstance and it promoted the characterization of historical periods by the distinctive features of their heroes. Thus the notion of the 'ages' of Cicero, the Church fathers, scholastic theologians, and Renaissance humanists came to supplement the notion of successive empires, for the emphasis on the "inward characteristics" of historical characters and their literary work promoted a cultural, rather than political approach to history. [2]

As Burckhardt saw it, "... an art of comparative biography arose which no longer found it necessary, like Anastasius, Agnellus, and their successors, or like the biographers of Venetian doges, to adhere to a dynastical or ecclesiastical succession. It felt itself free to describe a man if and because he was remarkable". As an early instance of the new historical perspective

---

[2] Erasmus' periodization of history is a good example: see above p. 35ff.; a critical, but balanced judgment on the humanists' contribution to the 'science' of history may be found in M. Ritter, *Die Entwicklung der Geschichtswissenschaft,* Munich and Berlin 1919, 128f.: "Zur Erklärung der alten Schriftsteller, sagt Erasmus, bedarf es der Kenntnis der Geschichte, des Staates, der Einrichtungen, der Sitten, alles Wissen der Alten. Dass solche Erkenntnisse, in genetischem Zusammenhang erfasst, geschichtlicher Natur waren und, wenn in die geschichtliche Darstellung aufgenommen, derselben eine unabsehbare Bereicherung zuführen mussten, liegt am Tage. Es war eine Anregung, wie sie in beschränkterem Sinne schon Augustinus gegeben hatte, als er zeigte, wie man die Würdigung des sittlichen und religiösen Charakters der Völker und im Zusammenhang damit ihre höchsten Gedanken von Gott, Menschheit und Natur in die geschichtliche Betrachtung aufnehmen könne. Aber ähnlich, wie damals, erhob sich sofort die Frage, ob die Jünger des Humanismus besser als die Nachfolger Augustins...zur Einarbeitung solcher Erkenntnisse in die geschichtliche Darstellung befähigt sein würden. ... Allein etwas anderes ist es, massenhafte Einzelzüge aus dem Leben eines Volkes in sich aufnehmen, und ein anderes, sie zur Einheit historischer Darstellung verarbeiten. Soweit Versuche letzterer Art gemacht wurden, zeigten sie doch, dass die Geister für diese höhere Aufgabe noch nicht gerüstet waren...

expressed in biographical collections Burckhardt mentioned Filippo Villani's *Vite* of illustrious Florentines : "Florence is here treated like a gifted family, in which all the members are noticed in whom the spirit of the house expressed itself vigorously". Turning to the 16th century, Burckhardt praised especially Vasari's *Vite* of the great artists. In view of the works mentioned by Burckhardt and some comparable ones such as Polydore Vergil's *De rerum inventoribus,* P. Crinitus' *De poetis Latinis,* L.G. Giraldi's *Historia poetarum tam Graecorum quam Latinorum,* one may conclude that here the superficially biographical order of preceding historical narratives based upon the succession of princes and prelates was abandoned in favour of intellectual biography and cultural history. Moreover, to a larger or lesser degree, these works embodied the principle of historical progress which was wholly absent from the medieval collections describing the lives of saints or heroes or from the alphabetical check-lists of heretics. In an age that gloated over its passions in Promethean imagery, the new biographical approach expressed the heroic ideal of a humanity that conquered history.

Burckhardt asserted that the new art of comparative biography took as its models the works of Suetonius, Nepos, and Plutarch; but unlike Georg Voigt [3] he did not treat biography as a mere subdivision of history. Later historians endeavoured to find in the Greek and Roman biographers the clue for the understanding of Renaissance biography. In so doing, they were greatly influenced by F. Leo's study of ancient biography. [4] To Leo biography was a literary genre which the Greeks had rigidly segregated from history until the syncretist scholars of Alexandria and Suetonius in Rome misused its traditional techniques for the purpose of composing history. Biography, as developed by the grammaticians of Alexandria, collected systematically such information as would help to form a judgment on the literary work of poets and scholars. However, the Alexandrine biographers neglected chronology and never attempted to integrate the details in a general picture. The limitations of their method were unhappily exposed when Suetonius in his *Lives of the Caesars* applied it to the writing of political history. To no avail did Plutarch at about the same time revive and adapt the older peripatetic manner of literary biography which analyzed actions and used chronology to achieve a measure of historical coherence sorely lacking in the Alexandrine fashion: the future belonged to the latter.

With the help of Leo's theories the historians of the Renaissance discovered all the Alexandrine shortcomings in the resolute "Suetonianism" of 15th and 16th century humanists, for it was wrongly assumed that only the Alexandrine style of biography could have taught the humanists how to

---

[3] G. Voigt, *Die Wiederbelebung des classischen Alterthums,* 4th ed., Berlin 1960, 2.501f. Voigt speaks of biography as the "favourite form" of humanistic historiography and emphasizes the "forceful emergence of personality" in the Renaissance age. However, this section is not yet contained in Voigt's first ed. published prior to Burckhardt's *Civilization.*

[4] F. Leo, *Die griechisch-römische Biographie nach ihrer litterarischen Form,* Leipzig 1901.

express the development of learning and culture. [5] E. Fueter, for one, went further and decided that the humanist preoccupation with biography only impaired the essential progress of historical study during the Renaissance. Almost contemptuously he asked:

> ... why did the humanists not go a step further, not replace their collections [of biographies] by books of real history and, for example, give a history of art in lieu of a history of the artists? No doubt the principal reason is that the weakness of their philosophical culture rendered them incapable of detaching abstractions—such as epic poetry or the Papacy—from their concrete representatives and conceiving them as objects of historical development. [6]

Typically, Fueter completed his critical discussion of the merits of Renaissance biography by lashing at the premise of Burckhardt's thesis, the emergence of individuality. The mere quantity of humanist biographies was no proof of the individualism of the Renaissance, Fueter suggested. Not one humanist biographer had matched Commynes' apprehension of the character of Louis XI. At any event, modern historical science could do without the maladroit portraits of humanistic biographers; it would reconstruct the very personalities from documentary sources. [7]

In the light of such assumptions, the question must be asked afresh: how did the humanists under the guidance of the ancient classics correlate or separate the genres of history and biography? Did the two genres afford them with a clear-cut alternative, since both were worked out in relation to very different models? If this were so, the scrutiny of humanistic biographies for values of history would not only produce meagre results, [8]—indeed it would be a mistake. [9] But the humanists did not, in fact, so neatly distinguish between biographical and historical techniques. Their treatises on the methods of historiography did include biography. [10] Suetonius and Plutarch were regularly described as historians, and so were, of course, Herodotus, Augustine and others whose influence can only have encouraged the humanists to abandon a straight annalistic and purely political approach to history. Thus, insofar as the humanists caught sight of a progressive history of civilization and attempted to write it, their efforts were neither exclusively inspired nor completely limited by the biographical method.

---

[5] Cf. E. Fueter, *Histoire de la historiographie moderne*, transl. E. Jeanmaire, Paris 1914, 112f.

[6] Ibid. 113.

[7] Ibid. 113.

[8] Cf. F. Stählin, *Humanismus und Reformation im bürgerlichen Raum; eine Untersuchung der biographischen Schriften des Joachim Camerarius*, Leipzig 1936, 43f.

[9] Under the influence of Leo's theories, M. Schütt (*Die englische Biographik der Tudor-Zeit*, Hamburg 1930, 11f., 18ff.) protested the improper treatment of biography "als Hilfsmittel für historische Forschung".

[10] *Artis historicae penus*, Basel 1579, 1.502 (Patrizi), 2.642f. and *tabula* (Zwinger); J. Bodin, Methodus ad facilem historiarum cognitionem, *Œuvres philosophiques*, Paris 1951, 259f.

Moreover, humanistic literature does not afford much evidence of an anti-thetical approach to the works of Plutarch and Suetonius. In fact, classical scholarship itself seems now ready to give up this approach together with Leo's formal distinction between peripatetic and Alexandrine biography. [11] As for Erasmus, the examination of his biographical writings will evidence his disregard for action and development and, consequently, his scant use of chronology, but his approach is motivated by his own fundamental views of history rather than by a superficial imitation of Suetonius. Suetonius cannot be said to have influenced him more than Plutarch for whom he had a profound admiration. Finally, Erasmus did, in fact, think in terms of specific representatives rather than abstract phases of civilization; but abstraction necessitates generalizations. What detained many humanists from further progress in this direction was, in spite of its recent disparagements, their high esteem of individuality. [12]

No discussion of the Renaissance may yet escape from examining the genesis of 'modern man', a minotaur, as it were, in the labyrinth of his self-conscious individuality. Fueter's formerly mentioned criticisms of the Burckhardtian concept of individualism in the Renaissance documented no more than the arrival of an anti-humanistic school of historians. Yet, even Burckhardt had second thoughts on the validity of his observations, though he preferred keeping them to himself. [13] Moreover, Burckhardt's critics in the matter of individuality included eminent historians who sympathized with his general approach to history such as Dilthey and Huizinga. [14] After half a century of research dedicated to the development of autobiographical writing, Georg Misch seems eminently qualified to pass a considered judgment on the question. [15]

We may recall Burckhardt's famous findings:

> In the Middle Ages both sides of the human consciousness—that which was turned within as that which was turned without—lay dreaming or half awake beneath a common veil. ... Man was conscious of himself only as a member of a race, people, party, family or corporation—only through some general category. In Italy this veil first melted into the air...; man became a spiritual *individual,* and recognized himself as such. ... [16]

Misch insists that Burckhardt's monolithic formula is still valid, but that its correct understanding depends upon some clarifications. To Misch it is obvious that the Middle Ages, as indeed all periods of history, are rich in personalities whose *actions* bear the marks of a singular, inimitable character.

---

[11] K. Ziegler in *Paulys Realenzyklopädie der klassischen Altertumswissenschaft,* vol. 21.1 (1951), esp. 909 (s.v. Plutarchos von Chaironeia).

[12] Cf. M.P. Gilmore, Individualism in Renaissance Historians, *Humanists and Jurists* 38-60.

[13] W. Kaegi, *Jacob Burckhardt, eine Biographie,* vol. 3 (Basel 1956), 717.

[14] Ibid. 713ff.

[15] G. Misch, *Geschichte der Autobiographie,* vol. 2 (Frankfurt a.M. 1955), 7ff.

[16] J. Burckhardt, *The Civilization of the Renaissance* 81.

But were they *conscious* of their individuality? First of all, he distinguishes what he terms "organic" or "biological" individuality from Burckhardt's concept of the *spiritual* individual. The various manifestations of an individual personality may be superficially connected in a psychological sense, in that they all originate from the same individual and contribute to our knowledge of that individual. On the other hand, they may exhibit a comprehensive structure of their own which attests to a personalized experience of the realities of life. [17]

Secondly, Misch notes that when true personality finds expression, it is not always focused upon an inner center of motivation. The core of his argument, then, is whether our actions and intentions converge into a focal point and whether or not this point lies within ourselves. [18] The latter distinction reveals, according to Misch, the fundamental difference between the Renaissance and the Middle Ages. Contrary to the self-centered individuality of the Renaissance, in the Middle Ages even a highly original, coherently personal course of action would be motivated by extraneous concepts stemming from widely accepted traditions. In claiming for the Renaissance a novel type of individuality rather than a vastly increased number of self-conscious individuals, Misch may actually be bolder than Burckhardt himself was. [19] If Misch's criteria are valid, they should apply to Renaissance biography no less than to the history of autobiography for which they were designed. The self-conscious individual may recognize in others the same interior center of gravity that he sees in himself. Erasmus certainly tried, and sometimes he succeeded. Even when he failed to recognize the central spring of an individual character, it would seem that he respected its existence. Yet his experience of individuality, as his experience of history, could hardly be called new. His originality rather lies in the determination and persistence with which he revived an ancient Christian tradition. With this frame of reference we may now approach the relevant passages in the work of Erasmus.

---

[17] G. Misch, *Geschichte der Autobiographie* 2.20f., 24.

[18] Ibid. 2.22: "...Vielmehr ist gerade die individuelle Einheit der Gestaltung ein Kriterium dafür, ob Lebensäusserungen, die durch ihre Zugehörigkeit zu einem und demselben Individuum nur psychologisch verknüpft sind, Ausdruck einer Persönlichkeit seien: überall, wo die Aeusserungen ein eigenes Gesamtgefüge haben, das ihnen individuelle Geschlossenheit, Einheitlichkeit, Form gibt, finden wir persönlichen Geist der Gestaltung. Wir sagen dann, die Wirklichkeit sei hier auf persönliche Art einheitlich erlebt. Aber wo diese Einheit nun ihren Ort habe, das ist nun die Frage. Nicht überall, wo persönlicher Geist sich ausdrückt, hat er auch seine Einheit aus sich selber. Hier liegen die grossen Unterschiede, deren fundamentalster der zwischen Mittelalter und Renaissance ist."

[19] Cf. W. Kaegi, *Jacob Burckhardt* 3.714.

II

When evaluating biography as a favourite field for humanistic historians, Voigt chose Petrarch's *De Viris illustribus* as a starting point.
"Petrarch", he said, "preferred to present Roman history in the form of
biographies rather than Livian narrative", and Boccaccio "followed suit"
with his collections *De claris mulieribus* and *De casibus illustrium virorum*. [20]
This statement glosses over a crucial point: Boccaccio's books, at least, did
not present a serious attempt to write Roman or other history. Essentially
they were collections of moralizing *exempla personarum,* often extolling
singular deeds rather than personalities. Such *exempla* offered personalized
illustrations of the basic virtues and vices exhibited by man as he braved the
whims of fickle Fortune or succumbed to her. As reference works such
books served the poets and orators of the next two centuries as well as the
historians, in fact, anyone intent at writing Latin prose in the humanistic
fashion and the tradition of classical eloquence.

It seems natural that Erasmus, the editor of *Apophthegmata* and *Adagia,*
would be favourably inclined towards the rhetorical effects resulting from
the adoption of *exempla.* The majority of his references to historical
characters, however, served both the demands of stylistic embellishment and
moral edification. Erasmus himself stressed this twofold purpose when
theorizing about the use of *exempla.* His youthful treatise on amplification
(*De duplici copia verborum ac rerum,* 1512) was a most appropriate place
for introducing the technique of exemplification. The desired end—persuasion with an ethical motive—was clearly pointed out in the following
formulation. "For the purpose of amplification", Erasmus wrote "examples
own a prime significance, if you wish to either discuss or admonish, to com-
fort, or commend, or blame; in short, if you endeavour to persuade, or to
move, or to cheer up." [21] The theoretical approach to exemplification was
resumed in Erasmus' manual of epistolography (*De conscribendis epistolis,*
1522) and again in the *Ecclesiastes* (1535). [22] Apart from a common
emphasis on the moral effect of *exempla,* not much consistency should be
expected from these passages, as exemplification is discussed each time
under a different aspect. It is, nevertheless, obvious that Erasmus' statements manifest a lack of interest both in defining an *exemplum* and in
logically analyzing its various modes of application. More important,
Erasmus' theoretical remarks on exemplification fail entirely to consider the
relationship between verbal expression and historical fact.

---

20 G. Voigt, *Wiederbelebung* 2.501, cf. 1.153.
21 LB 1 89C; cf. 1.93C.
22 LB 1.387ff.; 5.927D-F.

Aristotle in his *Rhetoric* had shown himself keenly aware of the fact that an *exemplum* referring to a figure of history must fulfil a historical function in addition to its rhetorical one. In view of this historical function Aristotle had tried to justify the rhetorical practice of exemplification logically by establishing two prerequisites. He had insisted that *exempla* taken from history should always be used in such a manner that the better known case explain the one which was less known: a specific action of some hero of the past should help to evaluate an as yet unfamiliar occurrence in the present or to substantiate a prophecy for the future. [23] In addition Aristotle had recognized that the effectiveness of historical *exempla* for the above purposes depended upon the cyclical recurrence of historical events, a theory which he accepted. [24]

It would seem that in their use of *exempla* the Renaissance humanists were not in the least restricted by the Aristotelian respect for the logic of history. Erasmus, for one, did not believe in historical cycles and among those of his *exempla* to be quoted on the following pages some will be found where well known instances are illustrated by obscure ones or remote cases by recent ones. In *De conscribendis epistolis* Erasmus followed, as he often did in these matters, the lead of Quintilian when he argued that a deed might be all the more remarkable and hence exemplary, if performed by a less distinguished person. [25] He also suggested that *exempla* should be chosen from either the most illustrious persons or those of either the remote past or domestic familiarity. Again he justified the use of *exempla* by purely moral motives: in their function of inflaming the mind with virtue examples from the oldest times are specially appropriate because they are too remote to evoke envy, whereas examples from among our personal circles have a natural appeal to our hearts. [26]

This matter merely illustrates what is otherwise well known: with his emphasis on the moral function of eloquence and on natural fluency rather than the systematic observance of rhetorical rules, Erasmus was indebted to the subjectivistic and activistic humanism of Cicero and Quintilian. [27] It is, however, interesting to notice a case where Erasmus chose a purely moral motivation even though Cicero himself felt urged to justify historically the use of the same example. In the opening passage of his dialogue *De senectute* Cicero confessed to the fictitious attribution of his speech to Cato and the exemplificatory value of that expedient: "... as there would be too little authority in a myth, we have attributed the whole discourse not to Tithonus, as Ariston of Keos did, [28] but to the aged Marcus Cato, so as to give the speech a greater authority". Yet Cicero insisted that this bit of

[23] Aristotle. *Rhetoric* 1.2.1357b, 1.9.1368a.
[24] Ibid. 2.20.1394a.
[25] LB 1.388B-D; cf. Quintilian, *Institutio oratoria* 5.11.5ff. (Erasmus borrows from the same passage in LB 1.92E-93A.)
[26] LB 1.387E.
[27] Cf. W. Rüegg, *Cicero und der Humanismus*, Zurich 1946, esp. 66ff.
[28] Cf. *Paulys Realenzyklopädie* 2.1.955.

biographical fiction did not offend the logic of history: "If it seems that he [Cato] argues more learnedly than he was wont to do in his own books, the credit should be given to Greek literature which, we know, he studied with great zeal during his old age". [29]

This passage was clearly in Erasmus' mind when he wrote the *Convivium religiosum*. For in reply to a quotation from *De senectute* one interlocutor warned that Cato's discourse, after all, was fictitious. Through the mouth of another interlocutor, Erasmus brushed aside the objection: there is really no great difference between Cicero's fiction and Cato's authentic words. One can imagine how Cato must have said similar things in conversation. "Tully was not so impudent as to depict Cato as other than he really was, nor, in his dialogue, to overlook decorum—an essential requirement in this kind of composition, especially when remembrance of that man was fresh in the minds of the writer's contemporaries". [30]

Cicero defended his biographical fiction with a historical fact: Cato's belated study of Greek literature. Not so Erasmus; the moral quality of decorum was, in fact, his only criterion to draw the thin line between legitimate freedom of expression and the improper use of examples. To say what precisely he meant by decorum is impossible, for the very vagueness of the term must have suited his own casual and unmethodical use of exemplification. At best, we can select from the mass of his *exempla* some typical cases which, he apparently felt, did not offend propriety.

Apparently it did not violate decorum if rhetorical amplification was used to stretch to the utmost the proving power inherent in an *exemplum*. Quoted out of context, the following findings on Plutarch could seem a conclusive characterization of that author resulting from a prolonged and penetrating study of his work: "... he was the greatest of classics, for he combined outstanding philosophical learning with the eloquence of a historian so that not only historical truth may be found in him, but also the authority and judgment of a most conscientious and learned philosopher". [31] Yet this is only a sample of commonplace formulas which, Erasmus suggested, could lend greater effect to a succeeding *exemplum* quoted from Plutarch.

Flattery too would not necessarily abolish the decorum required in the use of examples. Erasmus was an ingenious flatterer and a letter of May 1527 addressed to Sigismund I of Poland presents an appropriate specimen of his skill. The Polish king is hopefully extolled as the instrument of Providence, the saviour of war and misery stricken Europe.

> For normally in hopeless situations God is wont to suddenly intervene and bring forth from nowhere (*velut ex machina*) an individual endowed with singular virtue who reduces to calm the matter that had everywhere gone out of hand. Thus Camillus suddenly arose among the Romans who had fallen so low as to purchase their delivery with gold. And again when

---

[29] Cicero, *De senectute* 1.1.3.
[30] LB 1.682CD; the translation is C.R. Thompson's (*The Colloquies of Erasmus*, Chicago and London 1965, 66).
[31] LB 1. 89F-90A, cf. 387F-388A.

their situation seemed on the point of utter hopelessness, Scipio Africanus presented himself. So Moses was cast on the stage when the Hebrews in Egypt suffered continued and intolerable servitude. Thus Daniel appeared on the scene most unexpectedly when Susanna was in extreme danger... [32]

As to the prophet of so great a deed, Erasmus likens himself to aged Simeon. Joyfully he would conclude his day, if only God permitted him beforehand to witness the work of salvation.

Once, however, this captation saturated with pathos was brought to paper, Erasmus took pains to corroborate his exalted hopes by enumerating the political successes which Sigismund had accomplished in the past. His presentation of recent events in Polish history may today sound too optimistic, but then he may have relied upon some glowing description given to him by Polish acquaintances. Modern scholarship concurs with Erasmus' praise for Sigismund insofar as he preferred a reasonable peace to risky conquest. [33] As in the previous instance, taken out of context, some passages of the letter may rate as sober biographical history, but taken as a whole, the letter is an elaborate piece of flattery. Erasmus could not seriously ascribe a role to Sigismund which, he knew by then, not even a Charles V could accomplish. [34]

In writing this letter, Erasmus undoubtedly felt that he was serving a good cause. Therefore respect for decorum did not apparently conflict with a biographical interpretation that was, at best, wishful thinking. Yet, Erasmus' distortions never amount to outright disregard for the relevant facts of history, as may further be learned from his letter to Leo X in May 1515. In this prolific display of eloquent flattery Erasmus expressed at one point the expectation that this Pope alone would equal the combined virtues of the nine namesakes who preceded him in the Holy See. There follow short references, based on Platina, to the pontificate of each of the nine previous Leos. Some of these remarks offer not only sound but admirably succinct history, especially perhaps the "*felicem autoritatem*" ascribed to Leo I, the "*animum quoque ad utranque fortunam infractum*" credited to struggling Leo III, or "*simplicem illam et a Christo laudatam prudentiam*" attributed to Leo IV, the fortifier of Rome who rose from a lowly station and was credited with a number of miracles. On the other hand, the reference to Leo VI, "*pacis ubique sarciendae studium*", is typically Erasmian in emphasis and purposely contracted from a variety of commonplaces which Platina heaps upon a Pope who only ruled seven months and was virtually unknown. In the same way one hears of "*integritatem*" attributed to Leo VIII whose election was controversial and is now con-

---

[32] Allen 7.61.

[33] W. Pociecha in *The Cambridge History of Poland,* ed. W.F. Reddaway etc., Cambridge 1950, 1.321.

[34] Cf. below p. 71f. on Erasmus' criticism of the imperial policies leading to the Sack of Rome in the same year as the letter to Sigismund was written and on his disapproval of the subsequent political pact between Charles V and Clement VII; see also J. Huizinga, *Erasmus* ch. 17; R. Liechtenhan, Die politische Hoffnung des Erasmus und ihr Zusammenbruch, *Gedenkschrift*, Basel 1936, 152f.

sidered illegal. *"Sanctam tolerantiam"*, the quality ascribed to Leo V, presents a shrewd exercise in soft-pedalling, for a candid reference to the fact, frankly stated by Platina, that this Pope was overthrown after a short pontificate would have spoiled Erasmus' little game of flattery. [35]

In another sense, however, the juxtaposition of the ten Leos is more than a play. As a humanist, Erasmus was committed to *verba,* the art of verbal expression, rather than to *res* or *res gesta,* the scrutiny of facts. Time and again he showed himself alert to verbal assonances contained in the sound of a name. In rare cases this may have led him to employ *exempla* where the material nexus between the things and persons compared seems utterly lost in the accord of sound. [36] Frequently, however, the sound of a name conveys a message and spells out a moral obligation which the bearer of that name should honour. [37]

More cases in evidence will be presented shortly, but the case of the Leos already demonstrates the moral function of names. In the person of its bearer a name strikes a balance between *res* and *verba,* just as Erasmus' decorum strikes a moral balance between the facts of history and the words of eloquence, a balance between the real and the ideal. Erasmus once spoke of the *complexus ierum et verborum* by which the author may adjust a commonplace *exemplum* to his momentary requirements. By using appropriate language he may make up for the deficiencies of a matter or a person otherwise unfit for comparison. [38] At this point the observance of decorum became a crucial matter, lest the sole reliance on the *complexus rerum et verborum* license all sorts of demagogic practices. A page in the *Ciceronianus* permitted Erasmus to warn effectively against the abuse of historical *exempla.* He recollects a Lenten sermon which he once heard at Rome in the presence of Julius II. With sarcastic irony he records the general esteem in which the preacher is held: *"Romae Romanus ore Romano sonoque Romano"*. Yet his perfect oratory does not save the man from utter sacrilege. Despite the obvious lack of decorum Erasmus may be chuckling when he recollects how the preacher likened Julius II to *Jupiter Optimus Maximus,* brandishing the unfailing thunderbolt in his omnipotent hand. But then Erasmus expresses bitter contempt for an eloquence that adduces classical examples ranging from Iphigenia to Aristides and Scipio in order to reveal the heroism of Christ's death on the cross. [39] One recalls Scipio: Erasmus himself compared Sigismund of Poland to the hero of Rome. However, if Christ was compared to him, the same *exemplum* lacked the vital respect for decorum.

---

[35] Allen 2.84.
[36] Cf. Allen 1.342: Erasmus flatters Anne of Borsselen by comparing her to her three famous namesakes in antiquity. The name seems the only point in common between the four ladies and even there the identification is not supported by the ethymology. However, already the Romans had associated the semitic name of Dido's sister with the old-Latin goddess Anna Perennia.
[37] See below p. 70ff., 96.
[38] LB 1.388BC.
[39] LB 1.993B-E; for the importance which Erasmus attributes to decorum see also LB 1.987D and W. Rüegg, *Cicero und der Humanismus,* 94, 123 and passim.

III

In theory there exists a radical difference between the use of bio-graphical *exempla* for rhetorical purposes and a genuinely historiographic attempt to envisage and describe the characteristics of a person. In historical biography what matters is the balance of personal qualities that determines the individual and enlightens the events of his life-span; whereas exempli-fication, according to Aristotle, [40] singles out one quality which it uses as the term of comparison between two persons. The *exemplum* illustrates a preconceived concept of theoretical order; biography collects specific data towards the formation of a concept. Exemplification proceeds from the abstract quality of wisdom to the concrete case of Solomon; biography searches for the outstanding characteristics of Nero and diagnoses madness.

So far the theory; the practice in Erasmus' case, at any rate, fluctuates between the natural, inadvertent distinction and the effective pooling of the two modes. It is easy to find in his writings biographical *exempla* that are completely bare of any notion of character; yet it is hardly more difficult to find others that are not. The remarkable fact, perhaps, is that Erasmus developed his own technique to use exemplification as an efficient means for expressing his perception of personality.

With frank flattery Erasmus once recalled the outstanding properties of Henry VIII:

> Grateful for your devotion towards them, both Greek and Latin eloquence will never fail to mention that once there was a King Henry VIII of Britain who all in himself retained the gifts and distinctions of so many heroes, to wit, Ptolemaeus Philadelphus' zeal for the *bonae litterae,* the good luck of Alexander the Great, Philip's urbanity, the invincible will-power of Caesar, the sanity of Augustus, the gentleness of Trajan, the integrity of Alexander Severus..., [41]

and so on. As many of these characteristics return consistently when Erasmus described the English king, it is obvious that the famous rulers of antiquity are tossed in as topical illustrations of the preconceived abstracts. It will be recalled that Erasmus used the same technique of flattery in the example of the ten Leos; yet there he set out from historical personalities rather than the abstract virtues, and thus produced an exemplification that was historical rather than topical. However, in other passages following a similar pattern, Erasmus' subtle evaluation of individual style yields a

---

[40] Aristotle, *Rhetoric* 1.2.1357b.
[41] Allen 3.583.

summary characterization of the author. Even though taken from a formal preface in the high style, the following example may serve as an illustration:

> In Athanasius we admire the earnest and thorough perspicuity of his teaching; in Basil we embrace, besides his subtlety, a pious and suave eloquence. In his companion, Chrysostom, we grasp the spontaneous and copious profluency of speech. In Cyprian we venerate a spirit worthy of suffering martyrdom. In Hilary we admire the greatness of substance matched by the greatness of diction and, as it were, his cothurn. In Ambrose we love some appealing and penetrating judgments as well as the restraint which befits a bishop. In Jerome we rightly laud the rich store of Scriptural reminiscences. In Gregory we acknowledge pure saintliness unadorned by veneer (*fucus*)... But there is, I believe, no other author upon whom that bounteous and benevolent Spirit has showered his gifts more liberally than Augustine, [the author under consideration].... [42]

When taken by itself, each reference seems little more than an appropriately chosen formula, but the context woven from the single references commands a wealth of subtle emphasis and meaningful contrast. It is saturated with the appreciation of individual qualities in each father, although none of them is actually described as a personality.

What confirms one's rating of the above passage as evidence of Erasmus' perception of historical individuality is the consistency of the judgments here pronounced with other references to the same fathers. This argument, however, may in turn create new difficulties, for consistency of judgment is equally typical of the commonplace usage of *topoi*. For instance, nobody would credit Erasmus with a deeper understanding of Alexander the Great and his role in history, simply because he used that example, most regularly in fact, for handing down severe warnings to contemporary princes. There emerges a consistent image of Alexander's unbridled ambition and power-madness, [43] his failure to exploit his phenomenal good luck to anything better than bloody war and short-lived conquest, [44] his deafness to the voice of friendship and sane advice. [45] But if Erasmus reported how Colet in a sermon for peace "... further said, that they should imitate Christ, their own prince, rather than *Iulios et Alexandros,*" [46] the stark comparison of Christ with the ancient war-mongers on one hand and their matching namesakes in contemporary Rome on the other is topical to the highest degree. Moreover, one is bound here to realize that the Alexander *topos* is hardly one that Erasmus had coined himself on the basis of a thorough historical investigation.

---

[42] Allen 8.147; cf. Allen 6.470 on Athanasius: "Nihil habet durum quod offendit in Tertulliano; nihil ἐπιδεικτικόν quod videmus in Hieronymo; nihil operosum, quod in Hilario; nihil laciniosum, quod est in Augustino atque etiam Chrysostomo; nihil Isocraticos numeros aut Lysiae compositionem redolens, quod est in Gregorio Nazianzeno; sed totus est in explicanda re"; cf. also Allen 7.120; LB 5.912B-D.

[43] LB 2.871DE, 962A, 4.588F, 5.48EF, 559A; Allen 3.130, 5.359, 11.174.

[44] Allen 2.81, 206f.

[45] Allen 1.529f.

[46] Allen 4.525.

Consistency of expression, thus, may evidence either the formation of historico-biographical judgment or the adoption of a commonplace. It will shortly be shown that paradoxically, to the modern mind, Erasmus insisted that the two processes, far from excluding each other, were really one. Right now we must show that Erasmus still proceeded with consistency when expressing a highly complex opinion on a historical personality.

At the outset, one could challenge the consistency of Erasmus' judgment of Cicero. In *Convivium religiosum,* first published in 1522, Cicero was foremost among those true saints who were not to be found on the pages of the Christian calendar. The author of *De senectute, De amicitia, De officiis* was indeed "*afflatus coelesti numine*". Erasmus would much rather let the entire literature of scholasticism perish than the books of a single Cicero or Plutarch. [47] The *Ciceronianus* of 1528, on the other hand, criticized contemporary Ciceronians rather than the historical Cicero. Erasmus was anxious to prevent misunderstandings on this point, and yet the *Ciceronianus* offered an ironic reversal of the Cicero worship in *Convivium religiosum,* which no doubt affected the image of the great Roman himself. Now Erasmus spoke with grim humour of those who worship the "*deus eloquentiae*" like an Apostle in the calender and fill their houses with devotional likenesses of him. [48]

The apparent contradiction of the two statements dissolves, as we realize how Erasmus distinguished two opposing sets of values in Cicero's personality. From his early years to his last ones Erasmus continued unperturbed in his admiration for Cicero's moral philosophy. Accordingly, the Roman's polished style deserved similar praise as long as it was the worthy vehicle of his admirable ethics. But that same pen also betrayed the vanities and weaknesses of a human being and, at that, a rather imperfect one. Erasmus himself was aware of the consistency with which he had been judging Cicero, when he prefaced his 1523 edition of *Tusculanae Quaestiones*:

> ... Whether I matured with progressing age I don't know, but certainly since I came to love such studies Cicero has never pleased me more than now in my old age, not just for that heavenly style of his, but for the saintliness of his erudite spirit. ... What a vigour, what a wealth of wholesome and holy precepts, what a knowledge of and memory for old and recent histories. Further what deep thoughts about man's true happiness. ... Where Cicero's soul may dwell right now should perhaps not be pronounced upon by human judgment, but in the final balance I am favourably inclined towards those who hope that he is living the quiet life of paradise. ... [49]

---

[47] LB 1.682AB; cf. 1.677B; Allen 1.355ff., 4.65ff.

[48] LB 1.975A: "...Nosoponus: Non tantum in larario museoque, verum et in omnibus ostiis imaginem illius habeo belle depictam, quam et gemmis insculptam circumfero, ne unquam non obversetur animo. Nec aliud simulachrum in somnis occurrit praeterquam Ciceronis. Bulephorus: Non miror. Hypologus: Ego Ciceroni inter Apostolos in calendario meo locum dedi. Bu.: Nihil miror. Deum enim eloquentiae quondam appellabant."

[49] Allen 5.340, 338f.

Still in 1535 Erasmus wrote to a friend in Rome:

> ... I am being fancied as the enemy of Cicero and his implacable hater because I admire his genius and his profound erudition more than his eloquence. Yet I admire his eloquence so much as to admit in public, openly and heartily, that all those who are fluent by their own standards are silenced by the comparison with him. But something there is detrimental to his praiseworthiness. What wonder, if we regard Cicero as a human being, for God alone leaves nothing to be desired. ... [50]

The latter statement may be interpreted in the light of Erasmus' *Lingua* (1525) which shows how Cicero's accomplished prose also unveils the weakness of his character:

> Whoever rereads Cicero's *Orations* frequently will grow loath of them. ... Nobody could stand Cicero's facility and copiousness, if he were not so happy [in the choice of his words]; although he too has been called Asian [i.e. pompous]. And yet even those who approved of his expression and thought [*ingenium*] did not dare to trust the strength of his character, for the subject would have called for a steady and firm man. Demosthenes is considerably more succinct in his diction than Marcus Tullius and, nevertheless, the views of the latter are less widely acknowledged than his speech (... *tamen non tam probatum est pectus hominis quam oratio*). [51]

The last expression can be traced back to Augustine's verdict of Cicero: "*cuius linguam fere omnes mirantur, pectus non ita*". [52] Erasmus, however, gave a positive meaning to what the Church father said by way of criticism. For the Christian humanist Cicero's *ingenium* is divinely inspired although his character is inadequate. His language, however, exposes his merits and his faults with equal cogency.

As early as 1512 an ethical quality is praised in the orator Cicero when Erasmus commended his propriety in accusing Catilina. [53] Even in *Lingua* he found Cicero's "candour" laudable: the Roman uses his powers of persuasion only in favour of defendants, except for Verres, and there his very accusations are rather a defense of the province robbed by Verres. [54] Insofar as it is divinely inspired, Cicero's eloquence qualifies for comparison with the language of the great fathers. [55] But again his language—in fact only

---

50 Allen 11.178.
51 LB 4.671B-E; cf. LB 4.423AB: Cicero was shaking and sobbing like a child when he began a speech; LB 4.712A: he made immoderate use of jokes; however in Allen 9.131 wit is referred to as the greatest asset of Cicero's style.
52 Augustine, *Confessiones* 3.4.7.
53 LB 1.77A.
54 LB 4.712A: by contrast "Catonis eximias laudes nonnihil obscuravit, quod toties in ius vocavit et vocatus est".
55 Allen 1.332, 2.214: Jerome is paid the compliment that his style rivals that of Cicero; Allen 1.163: according to R. Agricola, Lactantius qualifies for the title of *Cicero Christianus*; Allen 11.207f.: "Mystica postulant suum quoddam dictionis genus. Quem, obsecro, ad pietatem accendit Lactantius? Atqui nihil eo nitidius. Dicas Christianum Ciceronem loqui, quanquam ille non tractat Scripturas, sed cum ethnicis digladiatur"; Allen 9.212: Cyprian and Augustine, could we ask them, would gladly admit the superiority of Cicero's style.

his language—betrays the shortcomings of the politician Cicero. It is typical of Erasmus' own limitations as an individual and a biographer that he never bothered to evaluate Cicero's active role in the Roman state. Only repeated comparisons with the younger Cato and Brutus, again on the basis of language, point in the direction in which Erasmus' sympathies run. Cato's verbal precision and directness warranted his finding Cicero ridiculous. [56] Brutus too scorned Cicero for provoking in his speeches those whom, once provoked, he cannot subdue. [57]

Both the consistency and the complexity of Erasmus' biographical judgments are also reflected by his references to Francis of Assisi. Erasmus himself emphasized the analogy to the case of Cicero: just as beloved Francis had to be defended against the Franciscans of Erasmus' own time, so had Cicero against the Ciceronians. [58] Yet, compared with the many-faceted Roman, single-minded Francis could hardly be called a complex individual. Erasmus respected the Saint of Assisi for his bonhomie (*"Franciscum semper existimavi bonum virum"*—*"minime malitiosum homi-nem"*). [59] Although Francis' *contemptus mundi* included the rejection of literary culture and the abhorrence of higher education, an attitude incompatible with the ideal of the new learning, [60] the single-minded foolishness of true Christianity was a paradox with which the author of *Antibarbari* had lived all his life. [61] In his hostility to worldly wisdom and temptations Francis could be associated with Socrates the sage as well as with Christ the fool. [62] Therefore, insofar as Francis' complexity reflected the paradox of learned ignorance it did not necessarily pose a biographical problem. The old Erasmus must no doubt be trusted when he repeatedly assured his readers that "...since I was a boy I've always had a sincere, reverent veneration for St. Francis, who by worldly standards was neither wise nor learned but was most dear to God by reason of his extreme mortification of worldly desires". [63] Erasmus' youthful devotion for St. Francis is corroborated by

---

[56] LB 1.980C, 4.712A; cf. 4.671E-672A.

[57] Allen 4.489; LB 4.665F-666A.

[58] LB 1.994CD.

[59] Allen 8.409; LB 1.994D; cf. 1.869A.

[60] LB 5.912CD: "In Francisco mirus omnium rerum, quae ad mundum pelliciunt, contemtus adeo ut nec ipse litteras discere voluerit, nec fratribus suis discendas permiserit, si prius eas non didicissent. Solitudinem autem non adfectavit, vel quia cupiebat omnes ad mundi contemtum adlicere, vel quia non instituebat agricolas, sed qui docerent populum, quibus esset data sermonis gratia, aut manuariis operis victum pararent, aut si nihil horum sufficeret, ad mendicitatem tanquam ad sacram ancoram confugerent. Si quis caeteros [sanctos] ad hunc conferat modum, reperiet omnes Deo fuisse caros diverso vitae genere, cum animorum natura fuerit diversa"; LB 1.871E: "Franciscum ... omnis literaturae rudem."

[61] Confessions of faith in Erasmus' work that betray a deep emotional involvement not seldom culminate in the citation of Christ's beatitudes or similar Scriptural texts; cf. LB 1.872D, 5. 140E; see above p. 40.

[62] LB 9.1219DE (quoted above p. 48f. n. 174), LB 5.566AB; cf. 4.498AB.

[63] LB 1.867E; the translation is Thompson's (*Colloquies* 505; it is not hard to see that the interlocutor Philecous may be identified with Erasmus; cf. the reference to his admiration for Rudolph Agricola); cf. Allen 7.22.

his often demonstrated familiarity with the legendary tradition of the Saint's life. [64]

It is exactly at this point, however, that Erasmus' comprehension of Francis was faced with another sort of complexity which bothered him even more than in the case of Cicero: in addition to the true legacy of St. Francis there existed a distorted image of the Saint, for which his own order was responsible. On one occasion, at least, Erasmus' polemics against contemporary friars and the worship of saints in general had come dangerously close to casting a shadow even upon the respectability of St. Francis. [65] In the last span of his life Erasmus became under heavy attack increasingly anxious to show the consistency of his faith in the true ideals of the historical Francis as well as his disgust with contemporary Franciscans who misrepresented the founder of their order merely to legitimize their greeds and idiosyncracies with his shining reputation. The progress of Erasmus' concern may be traced from a letter to Peter Mexia in March 1530 [66] to his colloquy *Exequiae Seraphicae,* first published in September 1531, and to a letter to Utenhove in August 1532, which reflects some recent criticism of the colloquy. Even the *Ecclesiastes* [67] of 1535 reasserts his view of the true, historical St. Francis. The colloquy is most articulate in spelling out the monk-made image of Francis: Christ converses with him as informally as with an old friend—(*"tam familiariter Christus cum illo fabulabatur?—Quid ni? Ut cum amico et sodali"*)—, when assuring him of a privileged entry into heaven for all his followers. [68]

The letter of 1532, on the other hand, states clearly Erasmus' view of the true St. Francis. One night the Saint appeared to him in a dream after midnight (this meant it was divinely rather than satanically inspired). The ragged, bare-footed figure is described in great detail: there is no trace of a meticulous, distinctive uniform and, more important, there is no trace of stigmatization. Francis has come to congratulate the slumbering humanist for scourging those same abuses which the Saint himself had always abhorred. He also names Erasmus a true friend of his order and announces his blessed end in the not so distant future: *"abiens dixit, dextra porrecta, milita strenue, brevi meorum eris".* [69] The last line, of course, brings to mind Erasmus' innumerable puns on the Franciscans and their superstitious

---

[64] LB 1.850EF, 5.52B, 566AB, 9.587AB; cf. LB 5.886B and 5.142F: "Franciscani Francisci sui traditiunculas adorant, amplectuntur, et quoquo terrarum se contulerint, secum circumferunt, tutos se non credunt, nisi libellus adsit in sinu."

[65] In the colloquy Πτωχοπλούσιοι (LB 1.739C): "Pandocheus: ...Ohe vos estis filii sancti Francisci. Soletis praedicare eum esse virginem, et ille habet tot filios? Conradus: Spiritus filii sumus, non carnis. Pan.: Infelix genitor ille. Nam quod in vobis pessimum est, animus est; corpore nimium valetis, planeque melius habetis in ista parte, quam expediat nobis, qui alimus uxorem et filias".

[66] Allen 8.405ff.; already the *Enchiridion* contrasted the true spiritual imitation of St. Francis with the purely superficial and technical one: LB 5.31DE.

[67] See above n. 60.

[68] LB 1.869D.

[69] Allen 10.80.

funeral practices. The Saint himself, it seems, respects an upright mind more than a corpse buried in the Franciscan cowl.

This passage is singularly expressive and highly typical of Erasmus' persistent attempts to present a realistic, enlightened—probably far too enligtened—portrait of the historical Saint: a portrait, moreover, which is sketched without enlisting the help of biography in the usual sense of the term. The peculiar deficiencies of Erasmus' 'true, historical' Francis are drastically exposed by a comparison with the eleventh *canto* of Dante's *Paradise*. Exactly like Erasmus, Dante honours a personal debt of love when vindicating the real Francis against the self-interested interpretations from among the Saint's own order. Like Erasmus, Dante does not make it easy for the modern reader to accept his vision of Francis: rightly or wrongly, he ignores certain features (in the case of Dante, they are the tender features which have endeared the image of the *Poverello* to generations of sensitive souls). But here the similarities end abruptly. Dante demonstratively bypasses the legendary tradition that must have loomed large in the imagination of Erasmus since he mentions Francis' sermon to the birds and chivalrous battles against the temptations of the flesh. [70] On the other hand, the Florentine poet buttresses his biographical study with short, specific references to the essential stations of Francis' life: his conversion resulting in a rift with his father, the successive approvals of his rule by Innocent III and Honorius III, the missionary expedition to Egypt, and, finally, the culminating imposition of Christ's stigmata (which adds the only miraculous touch to Dante's account). Francis' stigmatization is the only point where Dante's *vita* and Erasmus' description of character meet—and diametrically disagree. For Erasmus there is no life-span filled with development, there is neither young nor old Francis, there is no monk, no missionary, no mystic: there is merely the visual appearance of the Saint and an implication of individual character which, for the most part, remains ineffable.

In conclusion it may be said that in case of both Cicero and Francis Erasmus had mastered the enigma of personality to his own satisfaction. He succeeded in beholding their images, in the most literal sense, *sub specie aeternitatis*: Cicero was cautiously assigned a place in paradise and Francis was made to appear in the fullness of his true sanctity.

---

[70] See above n. 64.

IV

Whenever one compares Erasmus' scattered appraisals of one or the other historical character one is struck not only by his scant attention to biographical events and their chronological order but also by his static vision of the various characters. Erasmus' people are actors on the stage: they have roles, not lives, and each has just one role which, simple or complex, is unalterably his. He may act it well or he may act it badly but he cannot change the role in which he is cast, nor can he exchange it for another.

It may be that Erasmus' attitude reflected the influence of the ancient biographers. Both Plutarch and Suetonius approached historical characters with the Aristotelian terms of substance and quality. They neglected the notion of progress, which Augustine, the Christian, was to employ persistently in his analysis both of world history and his own life. Yet Erasmus' failure to observe the development of characters is not merely a matter of preference between various literary models. It is the logical consequence of his view of history and man's place in history.

This static view of personality is well illustrated by Erasmus' attitude to Augustine. In view of his famous autobiographical works the African father's life would appear to make a promising object of biographical inquiry and, moreover, to display a pattern whose central and crucial event is a conversion: the gradual transition from the dashing young dialectician and rhetorician to the saintly bishop and pious doctor. No such pattern, however, emerges from Erasmus' more or less comprehensive texts on Augustine. What Erasmus repeatedly emphasizes is not the conversion but, on the contrary, Augustine's probity previous to the conversion: "such was he that, even though he was still outside, those within [the faith] could consider him a good man in his own way". [71]

Through decades of continuous confrontation with some of the same contemporaries Erasmus often viewed their characters and actions with a constancy that ,were it more superficial, might be termed stubborn prejudice. His relations to Aleander illustrate this point well. Despite two public reconciliations, some ostensible praise for the curial diplomat, [72] and even

---

[71] Allen 8.148; cf. 8.128: "Talis quidam affectus [i.e.: quod omnes disciplinas prophanas simul et sacras suo stilo complecti studuit] habuisse videtur et divum Augustinum, quum adhuc esset in catechumenis. Et tamen videmus, vir alioqui coelesti praeditus ingenio quantopere frigeat in quibusdam progymnasmatis"; LB 5.41AB: "Divus Aurelius Augustinus, ut ipse de se in commentariis *Confessionum* suarum testatur, iam multo prius quam Christum indueret, contemserat pecuniam, pro nihilo habebat honores, gloria non commovebatur, voluptatibus autem usque adeo frena negarat, ut homo adolescens una muliercula contentus esset, cui et coniugii fidem servabat." On the other hand, see below, Appendix lines 61f., for a reference to changes conditioned by age in Augustine's literary work.

[72] In 1521 it was Erasmus who proposed a conciliation (Allen 4.460n.; cf. 5.204, 528), in 1532 it was Aleander (Allen 10.5ff.).

the inclusion of his name in a list of personal friends, [73] Erasmus never dropped his grave suspicions and regularly jumped at the conclusion that the Italian was playing foul. [74] Well aware of Aleander's talents, Erasmus was inclined to charge him with the composition of almost every well-written, but unsympathetic publication as soon as he, rightly or wrongly, suspected its author to conceal himself behind a pseudonym. [75] By a curious whim Erasmus would in his accusations often avoid Aleander's name, although making it clear whom he had in mind. [76]

In the same way, Erasmus' grateful love and respectful admiration for Henry VIII remained unshaken all the way through the king's divorce affair and well into his controversy with Thomas More. As late as the end of 1532 Erasmus commented on More's resignation from the chancellorship by explaining that he could not believe the rumours which had come to his ear:

> for I came to know the king's excellent character (*humanissimi Principis ingenium*), how steadily he continues to patronize the friends he once embraced and how unwilling he is to withdraw his favours from anyone, even though some human error may be pointed out in them. I also knew the sincerity of Thomas More and the dexterity of his conduct in the most crucial matters as well as in the most trivial ones. ... [77]

More's biographers treat it as a matter of course that Erasmus never wavered in his belief and affirmation of More's innocence. On the other hand, they blame Erasmus too readily for not having spoken out against the king. Yet, in either case, a change of character and the disavowal of an often shown integrity may have been equally inconceivable to Erasmus.

Erasmus' opinion of Clement VII may be chosen as a last example of the static nature which he ascribed to each individual. Clement's pontificate began in November 1522. Even at this point there might have been some good reason for Erasmus to doubt the new Pope's inclination towards his person as well as the ideals of Christian humanism. [78] Yet with an air of positive confidence, in January 1524, Erasmus addressed his first personal message to Clement. Despite the impression of flattery, this letter, the epistle dedicatory to his paraphrase of *Acts,* strikes a politely sincere, even bold key-note:

> ... Next, I applaud your adoption of the name *Clement,* for your temper is said to concur with it. But it is the surname of your family, *Medici,* that seems to me a singularly promising omen as hardly another name is better known throughout the world and more welcome. For grave and

---

[73] Allen 11.177.
[74] Allen 4.395f., 542, 5.34, 96, 112, 6.26, 35, 159, 380, 478f., 7.448, 8.454, 9.387, 403, 419; *Erasmi opuscula,* ed. W.K. Ferguson, 316f.
[75] Allen 6.351n., 7.12, 378, 541, 8.127f., 9.391, 398, 406, 442, 11.226.
[76] Allen 6.351, 354, 403, 478f., 9.33, 237, 398.
[77] Allen 10.135.
[78] A. Renaudet, *Erasme et l'Italie* 159ff.

deplorable diseases demand that fate appoints an illustrious doctor (*medicus*). ... In trusting hope all minds are now lifted up to the new *Medicen* as to some ἀπὸ μηχανῆ θεόν. O that God may deem us worthy of the fulfilment of this hope of his Christian people. [79]

Later in the year Erasmus repeated: "...and it is Clement's duty to respond to his name". [80] The Pontiff had not yet made history, but history had set out for him a task to which he might or might not live up. One way in which this task was translated into practice may be learned from another letter of the same half year. Erasmus confessed uncertainty as to whether Clement had renewed or abandoned his predecessor's anti-French alliance with Spain. However that might be, nothing befitted a Pope less than political deals. Rather he ought to be the father of all and to work for concord. [81]

For several years Erasmus continued to express satisfaction both with the way Clement treated him personally and with the Pope's approach to world affairs. [82] When, in 1527, the news of the Sack of Rome reached him, Erasmus reacted with deep regret and disgust and expressed these feelings as frankly as could be expected of anyone committed to the Imperial court. At the beginning of October he voiced his grief in a letter to Sadoleto: Rome, the fortress of the Christian faith, the quiet home of the Muses, the mother of all nations, Rome had been mishandled more savagely this time than during any of the barbaric invasions of antiquity. The Pope had shared the fate of his city: "*vidimus Ecclesiae principem Clementem inclementissime tractatum*". [83] The expression is undoubtedly meant to convey more than just an elegant pun. Clement's name symbolized a specific moral obligation. If the bearer had to honour this obligation, so had his enemies and judges. Consequently, the Emperor could not go free of blame, nor could, in fact, the Pope himself for he too had at this occasion failed to play his role properly. In August 1527 Erasmus addressed Archbishop Lasky in the epistle dedicatory of an edition of Ambrose. Any contemporary would guess what unfavourable comparison was foremost in Erasmus' mind, when he recalled how the great bishop of Milan had braved the unjustified wrath of an Empress:

> Ambrose..., however, was not in the least frightened. 'I shall not', he said, 'give up to the wolves the flock in my charge. Kill me right here, if you wish'. But nobody can act the part of Ambrose, unless he be prepared

---

[79] Allen 5.390; the letter was written after Erasmus had received encouraging news from his trusted and well-informed correspondents in Rome.

[80] Allen 5.527; cf. the colloquy Ἰχθυοφαγία (1526) LB 1.793C, 794D; Allen 7.511.

[81] Allen 5.396.

[82] Allen 6.88, 311: "Pontifex cohibuit suos ne pergerent stringere calamum in Lutherum, et sapit"; Allen 5.543, 6.480: "Clemens septimus bis iam misit ducentos florenos, nihil non pollicens"; cf. also Allen 6.125f.: Clement's dispensation enabling Erasmus to make a will, addressed to "Dilecto filio Erasmo de Roterodamis, magistro in theologia".

[83] Allen 7.509f.

to die in the fulfilment of his pious duty. It would even seem exceedingly difficult that anyone could earnestly act the part of a priest when actually he likes other parts better (*Imo difficillimum est cuiquam vere sacerdotem agere, qui libenter aliud est quam sacerdos*). [84]

Not now, however, would Erasmus pass a final judgment on Pope Clement. As late as August 1528 he exclaimed hopefully : *"utinam hic saltem sit summus Pontifex vel, ut melius dicam, opt. maximus"*, and he wished Clement success for the attempted mediation between France and Spain. [85]

Hereafter, Erasmus' sympathy for Clement faded quickly. He came to believe that the new accord between Pope and Emperor reflected nothing but political expedience; he also formed a dark suspicion that Clement was secretly encouraging his enemies. [86] His final verdict on Clement, however, resulted from yet another event. In August 1530 the last episode of Florentine democracy ended in defeat and surrender. In the heart of the Medici Pope self-interest had won out. He had conclusively failed to fulfil his historical mission. It is always the suppressor of Florence whom Erasmus called indignantly the "inclement Clement" [87] To judge from the preserved letters, he all but ignored the Pope during the last years of his pontificate and did not deem him worthy of any commemoration after his death.

It is important that Erasmus' experience of Clement be presented in the way he himself had understood it. He never said that Clement ceased to be his former self or that he, Erasmus, had changed his mind about the Pope. Rather it became increasingly evident to him that the historical Clement fell categorically short of the Clement who ought to have been, as the Pope did not face up to the perennial dignity of his holy office and the standing promise of his personal name. Clement's case thus evinces again the crucial point that, in Erasmus' view, personality was determined by an individual but static function. The consciousness of such a central function in his own life made Erasmus cling to all the principal views of his early years. It made him reject the bulk of the adjustments proposed to him from various sides. Unlike his friend Thomas More, Erasmus did not conclude that under changing circumstances the substance of his personal role was bound to change.

---

[84] Allen 7.123.

[85] Allen 7.450 to Cricius: "Pontifex dicitur esse Niceae, ea est Sabaudiae civitas maritima: aiunt eum moliri concordiam inter Gallos et Caesarem. Utinam hic saltem sit summus Pontifex vel, ut melius dicam, opt. maximus! Sed Iulio ad bella provocanti facile obtemperatum est; vereor ne non perinde mos geratur huic ad pacem hortanti, si tamen hoc agit quod iactatur"; Erasmus' relative friendliness may in part be due to the Pope's recent brief in his favour: Allen 7.105f.; cf. 148. However, a week after the letter to Cricius, he sounds less hopeful: Allen 7.468.

[86] Allen 8.325, 9.26-28, 251, 370; LB 5.360B (*Consultatio de bello Turcico*, March 1530): "Orandum est atque etiam sperandum est, fore ut nostri misertus Dominus Jesus vicario suo Clementi VII mentem inserat ipso dignam...".

[87] Allen 9.27, 170, 243.

72

Whenever Erasmus encountered personalities he became at once concerned with their definitive character, the central motor which propelled their sundry thoughts and actions. But often, perhaps more often than not, he could not make it out. The gigantic figure of Martin Luther signals one of his most intensive struggles and dramatic failures to solve the central enigma of personality. [88]

Some elements of continuity in Erasmus' judgment of Luther can nonetheless be observed. From the outset Erasmus noted that Luther's emergence was not motivated by personal ambition or avarice, [89] and there is no evidence that he later departed from his early trust in Luther's personal integrity. A slanderous allegation of premarital incontinence, once made, was quickly dropped and even denied; [90] it thus remains the exception which confirms the rule. According to another primal conviction of Erasmus, Luther had a sound theological training [91] and was essentially right in his criticism of corrupted religious practice and scholastic distortions of the Christian faith. Despite his later anxiety to indicate a basic divergence in the reforming approaches of Luther and his own Christian humanism, Erasmus never denied a common point of departure. It did not escape Erasmus that those who rejected Luther's stand categorically were bound to repudiate the *raison d'être* of Christian humanism too; hence he kept insisting that Luther's enemies were worse than Luther himself. [92]

Nevertheless Erasmus repeatedly indicated an element of change in Luthers' attitude. Initially he had commended Luther for speaking his mind

---

[88] Cf. Allen 4.101 (October 1519): "De spiritu hominis [i.e. Lutheri] non ausim iudicare: est enim difficillimum, praesertim in partem peiorem"; in the same vein Erasmus still writes in January 1521: Allen 4.441: "De spiritu illius nolo, nec meum est, ferre sententiam." The incertainty which Erasmus felt about his judgments of Luther is well documented by his reaction to Luther's letter of April 1524 (Allen 5.444ff.), delivered to him by Joachim Camerarius. On 3 June 1524, Erasmus reports to Pirckheimer: "Scripsit ad me Lutherus; sed suo more, pollicens se ignosciturum imbecillitati meae, si modo ne ex professo scribam adversus illius dogmata. Illi respondi, sed paucissimis, ac meo more civiliter" (Allen 5.469). Probably after renewed and intensive efforts to analyze Luther's letter, Erasmus writes again to the same Pirckheimer on 21 July 1524: "Scripsit ad me Martinus Lutherus per Ioachimum quendam satis humaniter. Cui non sum ausus pari humanitate respondere propter sycophantas. Respondi tamen paucis" (Allen 5.494).

[89] Allen 3.530, 540, 4.103.

[90] Allen 6.187 contains a friendly reference to Luther's bride: "...puellam mire venustam ex clara familia Bornae, sed, ut narrant, indodatam". However, in Allen 6.199 Erasmus adds to a similar reference that the bride gave birth a few days after the wedding. He repeats the same story in Allen 6.240 and 242, but rejects it in Allen 6.283f.: "De coniugio Lutheri certum est, de partu maturo sponsae vanus erat rumor; nunc tamen gravida esse dicitur. Si vera est vulgi fabula Antichristum nasciturum ex monacho et monacha, quemadmodum isti iactitant, quot Antichristorum milia iam olim habet mundus!"

[91] While Erasmus' respect for Luther's theological knowledge remained unchanged, his understanding of Luther's theology varied. Allen 4.105 (October 1519): "...quod scholasticis dogmatis non tantum defert quantum Evangeliis..."; Allen 4.544 (July 1521): "Utinam vir ille tantum haberet moderationis quantum habet eruditionis theologicae!"; Allen 6.288 (March 1526): "... Luterus data opera pertraxit omnia ad scholasticas argutias, quod in his sciat me minus exercitatum"; cf. LB 9.871E.

[92] Allen 4.490f.; cf. below n. 100.

freely, [93] but his admiration and support of the German friar ended after the publication of the *Babylonian Captivity*. He felt that Luther's language had bypassed mere candour and now displayed the same lack of moderation as characterized his detractors, who were for the most part Erasmus' own opponents. As unrefrained arrogance smothered the basic truth of his message Luther sank to the level of his enemies. [94] From 1524 onward, however, Erasmus perceived in Luther a new turn to moderation. Even though he insisted that it was Luther himself who had changed (*"Luterus nunc mitior esse incipit, nec perinde sevit calamo"*), [95] the observation clearly occurred to him by way of contrast with some yet more radical manifestations of the protestant spirit. At first it was the Peasants' War that made Luther look conciliatory by comparison. [96] A few years later Erasmus observed that the obstacle in the way of sanity was not Luther so much as Zwingli, Oecolampadius and Capito. [97] All through 1528 Erasmus kept insisting that the "Lutheran fever" was ebbing. He repeatedly spoke of Luther's "palinodes", and even noted that the reformer had fallen silent. [98] The change in Luther's attitude confused Erasmus and frustrated his efforts to conceive a coherent and monocentric picture of the German reformer. What confused him even more was that his own observations lacked a clear perspective; try as he would, he could not coordinate them into a single focal point. As early as 1521 he was unwillingly aware of a change in his own judgment of Luther. In writing to Jodocus Jonas he wondered whether at any time in the past the study of sacred letters and Christian morals had lain in greater abjection:

> Pious minds, to whom nothing is more important than the glory of Christ, groaned at the sight of this. And the result was that in the beginning Luther had as much approbation on all sides as, I believe, has come to any mortal for several centuries past. For, as we easily believe what we ardently desire, they thought that a man had arisen who, free from all the attachments of this world, could bring some remedy for such great evils. Nor was I entirely without hope, except that immediately at the first

---

[93] Allen 3.409 (October 1518): "Eleutherium audio probari ab optimis quibusque; sed aiunt illum in suis scriptis sui dissimilem esse. Puto illae conclusiones placuerunt omnibus..."; Allen 3.540 (April 1519): "Quaedam admonuit recte, sed utinam tam feliciter quam libere!"; Allen 3.609 (May 1519): "Optimi quique amant libertatem Lutheri cuius prudentia non dubito quin cautura sit ne res exeat in factionem ac dissidium".

[94] Allen 4.374 (November 1520): "Lutherus etiamsi vera scripsisset omnia, tamen eo modo scripsit ut veritati suum fructum inviderit"; Allen 4.399 (December 1520): "Lutherus in dies scribit atrociora..."; Allen 4.487 (May 1521): "Quod si vera fuissent omnia, id quod aiunt longe secus habere qui sciptorum illius censuram agunt, provocatis tam multis quis alius exitus expectari poterat quam hic quem videmus?"

[95] Allen 6.240; cf. the following n.

[96] Allen 5.434 (April 1524): "At nunc Lutherus scribit in se ipsum, videns rem alio vergere quam putarat, et exoriri populum non Evangelicum sed diabolicum..."; Allen 5.543 (September 1524): "...video sub praetextu Evangelii subnasci novam gentem, procacem, impudentem et intractabilem—breviter talem ut nec Luterus ipse ferat...".

[97] Allen 8.473; cf. 8.113.

[98] Allen 7.367, 422, 497, 516; in his later statements on Luther, however, Erasmus failed to notice any moderating tendencies: cf. Allen 10.384, 11.21, 134.

sampling of the tracts which had begun to appear under Luther's name I was quite afraid that the matter might end in tumult.... Perhaps someone will ask whether I have another mind regarding Luther than I had formerly. No, indeed, I have the same mind. I have always wished that, with changes made of certain things which were displeasing to me, he discuss purely the Gospel philosophy... [99]

Even now Erasmus did not deceive himself with regard to the many basic concerns that he shared with Luther. As Luther, however, proceeded to discredit and destroy the very good that lay in his teaching, he would necessarily wreck the reforming hopes of Christian humanism as well. In 1522 Erasmus wrote:

It cannot be denied that Luther came up with a very good story and that all the world applauded him wholeheartedly when he took in hand the affairs of nearly-forgotten Christ. Would that he handled so great a matter by applying to it more weighty and more reasonable measures.... And, in turn, would that there were in his writings not so many excellent points or that he did not wreck them with harmful ones which are quite unbearable. [100]

How could anyone retain a clear judgment if there was clearly more than one Luther? In April 1524 Erasmus noted that "Luther was now writing against himself", [101] and in March 1526 he wrote:

I am intrigued to perceive in Luther two so very different persons (*personas*). Certain things he writes in such manner that one feels the breathing of an apostolic bosom; but then, again, is there a buffoon whom he would not outdo with his bons-mots and his grimaces, with his insults and gibes? ... as if he had completely forgotten in what kind of play he was acting and what sort of mask (*personam*) he had donned. [102]

Failing to find within Luther the coveted master key to the comprehension of his actions, Erasmus escaped from the riddles of individuality to a

---

[99] Allen 4.487, 493, quoted in J.C. Olin's translation (*Christian Humanism and the Reformation, Desiderius Erasmus*, New York 1965, 152, 163). In the same confused letter Erasmus suggested he might in the past have written differently, had he anticipated the results of Luther's action (Allen 4.492); but on this point he again contradicted himself: Allen 7.497. Erasmus further admitted to a change in his judgment of Luther as well as in that of many others: Allen 5.602ff.; LB 9.379AB, 388BC.

[100] Allen 5.126; cf. Allen 4.497: In this letter to Warham (May 1521) Erasmus used stunning words to express his alarm at the doom of Christian humanism between the Scylla of Luther's radicalism and the Charybdis of the monkish reaction: "Vellem Lutherus aut tacuisset quaedam aut aliter scripsisset. Nunc vereor nec si vitemus hanc Scyllam ut incidamus in Charybdim multo perniciosiorem. Si istis qui ventris ac tyrannidis suae causa nihil non audent, res succedit, nihil superest nisi ut scribam epitaphium Christo nunquam revicturo"; Allen 5.251 (Spalatin's translation): "Wenn der Luther solt zu poden geen, so wurd wider keyn Gott noch keyn mensch mit den munchen kunnen auszkummenn. Folgend, so kan der Luther nicht umbkümmenn on das es vergee dann mit im ein grosser teyl der Evangelischenn lautterckeit"; cf. Allen 5.276, 330.

[101] See above n. 96.

[102] Allen 6.285; cf. 6.276.

typological interpretation. If Luther was not to be apprehended as a self-centered individual, at least he could be understood as a tool in the hands of those supramundane powers that welded human destiny and history. This solution satisfied, even fascinated, Erasmus. In the formerly quoted letter to Jonas (10 May 1521) he is found asking:

> And I greatly wonder, my dear Jonas, what god has stirred up the heart of Luther, in so far as he assails with such licence of the pen the Roman pontiff, all the universities, philosophy, and the mendicant orders. [103]

The phrase *"vehementer demiror..., quis deus agitaverit pectus Lutheri"* no doubt is a commonplace, but one that is pregnant with meaning. It is as if Eramus were to specify his first expression when, four days later, he asked in view of Luther's undertaking and following: "what *cacodaemon* admixed that seed of the worst kind to the affairs of mortals". [104] That seed was sprouting in the Peasants' War when Luther himself, in Erasmus' words, "must recognize that the matter turns out far different from what he had anticipated and that not an Evangelical race is emerging, but a satanical one". [105]

Yet at other times Erasmus felt that it was really God, not Satan, who possessed Luther and staged the Reformation tragedy to his own satisfaction. In September and again in December 1524, while still groping for the meaning of the perplexing current events, Erasmus called Luther a "necessary evil (*necessarium malum*, ἀναγκαῖον κακόν)". He also spoke of him as a "medicine; though it was bitter and violent, I hoped it would bring a certain measure of good health to the body of the Christian people". [106] One notes that this early dawn of a new understanding occurs simultaneously with Erasmus' diagnosis of a moderating trend in Luther's own writing but, ironically, after the humanist had finally taken the pen against the reformer and thus unleashed a personal controversy which in due course would cause him new torrents of bitterness. Nevertheless, the quoted statements announce the more hopeful mental frame of the later Erasmus. They belong to the imagery expressing his concept of world history which has been examined in the first part of this study. Luther, along with the Pharaohs and Nebuchadnezzars of old, is the horrible instrument in the hand of the life-saving surgeon. Luther—as well as Erasmus and everybody else—is for the short span of his mortal existence an actor in God's historical

---

[103] Allen 4.487 (Olin's translation, *Desiderius Erasmus* 152); cf. Allen 5.594: "Quid Luthero suus dictet spiritus, ipse viderit".

[104] Allen 4.494.

[105] See above n. 96.

[106] Allen 5.543, 590; these expressions contrast sharply with the way Erasmus was using the same metaphor a little earlier: Allen 4.494 (May 1521): "Et ecce incendium Decretalium, Captivitas Babylonica, Assertiones illae nimium fortes reddiderunt *malum*, ut videtur, *immedicabile*"; and a very similar phrase: Allen 5.28; cf. also above n. 100.

mystery-play. [107]   With the birth of this imagery the Luther dilemma ceases to be a vexing, unsolvable puzzle.   But the solution thus conceived, though certainly falling within the frame of Erasmus' historical thought, is not a biographical one.   Erasmus was never to resume the sequence of brilliant biographical sketches which he had undertaken before the Lutheran tempest broke.

Thus the incessant preoccupation with Luther plunged Erasmus into a whirlpool from which he was finally to emerge with his own peculiar concept of history; first, however, the Luther impasse halted his willingness to read characters.   As did the real Luther, so would the Luther of Erasmus' imagination draw other characters into the surge of his action until their own historical identity was obscured beyond recognition.   Reuchlin may here serve as an example.   Within a week from turning out the bull *Exsurge Domine* against Luther, Rome had, in fact, pronounced its final censure of the views of Reuchlin.   At best, Erasmus saw in Reuchlin the symbol of Christian humanism and the immediate victim of Luther's impertinence. [108] This was the Reuchlin who assisted Erasmus in his labours over the great edition of Jerome's works and for whom he set an unforgettable memorial in the colloquy *Apotheosis Capnionis*.   At worst, however, he saw Reuchlin as a sectarian just like Luther, another leader of one of those factions that disrupted the unity of Christendom and imperilled the orderly progress of reform. [109]

The case of Luther stands out, but other characters further back in history confronted Erasmus with an analogous problem of assimilation. There is some indication that he was fighting a long and losing battle for a consistent appreciation of Augustine.   When work on Froben's edition of the African father was far advanced, Erasmus approached, in the spring

---

[107] On Allen 5.605 see above p. 29; cf. 6.275f.: "Quin insuper addebat nonnihil laeti ominis ipsum Lutheri cognomen, quod Germanorum lingua 'repurgatorem' sonat. Id habet ex patris opificio, qui rudes aeris massas officina sua repurgat. Augebant theatri favorem inepti tumultus quorundam, qui protinus moliebantur exsibilare coeptam fabulam... . Iam et illud arguebat hoc negocium aliquo numine geri, quod quo magis in adversum nitebantur coniuratae phalanges et his favens monachorum potentia, hoc latius serpebat malum. ... Ego inter applausores et exibilatores medius ex multis coniecturis divinavi rem in seditionem exituram. ... Una spes adhuc superest. ... Si forte meruit hoc mortalium impietas, ut per tales homines perque tam saevum chirurgum curaretur, quando malagmatis, potionibus et emplastris sanari non poterat, spero futurum ut quos Deus afflixit rebelles, consoletur resipiscentes.   Solet enim nonnunquam populi sui peccata per Philistaeos et Holophernas et Nabugodonosoras emendare..." cf. Allen 8.111.

[108] Less than three months after the bull *Exsurge Domine* had been issued and Reuchlin had been silenced, Erasmus wrote on 9 September 1520 that Luther's lack of moderation enraged the princes and especially Pope Leo.   "Iam Capnionem rursus aggrediuntur tantum odio Lutheri: qui me dissuadente nomen illius suo negocio admiscens, et illum degravavit invidia, et sibi nihil omnino profuit" (Allen 4.339)   Shortly afterwards Erasmus wrote to Leo X in defense of Reuchlin and himself: "Esse video qui... conati sunt causam bonarum literarum, causam Reuchlini meamque causam cum Lutheri causa coniungere, cum his nihil sit inter se commune" (Allen 4.344f.); the statement is repeated in a letter to Reuchlin: Allen 4.372.

[109] Allen 4.538: "Neque Reuchlini neque Lutheri factioni me unquam admiscui; Christi gloriae pro mea virili semper favi"; cf. Allen 4.372n.

of 1528, the Flemish theologian Gerard Moringus with the request that he supplement the new edition with a suitable biography of its author. Moringus' reply expressed surprise that Erasmus should see unfit to repeat for Augustine what twelve years earlier he had so brilliantly accomplished in his biography of Jerome, similarly written for one of Froben's great patristic editions. As Moringus pointed out, such a labour of love from Erasmus' pen might allay some suspicions of his true feelings for Augustine. Moringus had, in fact, been planning a biography of Augustine but had dropped the project upon the news of the Froben edition being prepared by Erasmus, or so at least he wrote. [110] Thus, when a year later the first volume of Froben's *Augustine* appeared, it contained no satisfactory biography, a fact that must have prompted Moringus to resume his own efforts. [111]

Erasmus' embarrassed move to accompany the Augustine edition with a tradition-hallowed and conveniently selective *encomium* rather than an analytical and emcompassing biography is not surprising. In composing the *Hieronymi vita* Erasmus had largely drawn on the father's own letters. In Augustine's letters, on the other hand, he found disappointingly little personal detail and a versatility that defied characterization. [112] He regularly consulted Augustine's views and seemed forever torn between admiration and anger, praise and blame. There is a measure of ambivalence in his judgments on Augustine's eloquence [113] and scholarship [114] as well as in his opinions on Augustine's exegesis [115] and attitude to heresy and war. [116] In

---

110 Allen 7.396f.

111 See Allen's introductory n., 7. 396; as an appendix to his first volume Erasmus printed the *Life of Augustine* by Possidius of Calama.

112 See below p. 87 and Appendix, lines 28ff.

113 Cf. Allen 4.26: "Porro cum olim Africa permultos aediderit eloquentia doctrinaque celebres, inter quos sunt in primis Tertullianus et Augustinus, tamen vix ulli contigit Rhomanae dictionis germana puritas praeterquam Cypriano"; Allen 8.153: "Habet enim Augustinus suum quoddam dicendi genus, argutum et periodis in longum productis multa convolvens, quod lectorem et familiarem et acutum et attentum et bene memorem requirit, denique tedii laborisque patientem, quales non ita multos reperias"; LB 5.857BC: "Augustinus in hoc genere extemporali felix et argutus. Quod autem dulcior est quam gravior, quod numeris ac similiter desinentibus gaudet, quodque crebris digressionibus moratur auditorum animos, suae gentis ingenio tribuit vir pius et humanus."

114 Erasmus frequently notes Augustine's limited knowledge of Greek and his ignorance of Hebrew: e.g. LB 5.77E; Allen 3.438: "Augustinus eximius doctor est, sed cum nullo Graecorum conferendus"; in some lengthy statements on Augustine's scholarship one notices at times a rather negative tenor (Allen 3.334ff.), at times a more positive one (Allen 8.153f., LB 10.1730ff.).

115 Allen 7.120; nobody is "nodis explicandis argutior" than Augustine; cf. 8.150. On the other hand: Allen 8.432: "Augustinus non indiligenter tractavit hanc provinciam [commentarios in Psalmorum opus]; nisi quod permulta dare cogitur auribus populi quem instituebat, occupato doctoque lectori non admodum necessaria, nonnunquam et onerosa"; LB 6.477D: "Siquidem existimamus et Augustino prophetiae donum adfuisse in explicandis Sacris litteris, et tamen alicubi non assequitur sensum Scripturae germanum."

116 LB 5.800BC: "Similiter divus Augustinus rhetoricam ac philosophiam in paganismo didicit, in haeresi Manichaeorum exercuit. Neutrum illi ademit Spiritus, sed quod erat imperfectum absolvit, illud etiam ipsum quod in eo sceleratum erat vertens in lucrum Ecclesiae. Nisi enim aliquando cum Manichaeis insanisset, nec tam evidenter

78

later years Erasmus may have outgrown the youthful boldness of some criticism that he had once defiantly thrown Augustine's way; on the other hand, he could not forgive the Church father his small consideration for Free Will, for this embarrassed Erasmus in the controversy with Luther. In a general way his frequent readings of Augustine seem to have inspired in Erasmus a certain awe for the father's ebullience and profundity. This awe, however, differed fundamentally from his congenial sympathy for Jerome. [117] Thus his dilemma in view of Augustine remained obvious to all and his lack of enthusiasm continued to offer a target for criticism from all sides. [118]

V

With the examined cases in mind, it seems possible to suggest some conclusions about Erasmus' understanding of individuality and about the role of personality in his concept of history. These findings should prepare the way for a concluding examination of the small, but substantial body of Erasmus' fully developed biographical portraits as well as a tentative indication of the place this body of writing may have filled within his life-work and the general history of biography.

Erasmus seems firmly committed to see the figures of past and current history as spiritual individuals whose thoughts and actions, while often very complex, were nevertheless focused upon a center of gravity that lay within themselves. His trouble was that it proved exceedingly difficult to under-

---

prodidisset nec tam efficaciter redarguisset illorum insaniam"; Allen 8.151: Augustine fights heresy "solo gladio Spiritus ..., licet adversus Donatistas et Circumcelliones, quoniam ipsi ferro rem gerebant; cf. Allen 4.489, 9.155. On the other hand, see LB 6.319F-320B (commenting on Luke 22.36): "...Tolerabilior erat interpretatio, si ad hunc modum intelligamus, etiamsi quando adsit defendendi facultas, tamen abstinete a defensione, solo verbi Divini gladio vos defendite. Hic frigidissimam distinctionem afferunt quidam, iussit habere gladium ad defensionem, vetuit promi ad vindictam. Iam illud videndum, an de bello sibi satis constet Augustinus: qui cum tot locis Christiane bellum detestetur, nunc adversus Manichaeos ac Donatistas belli patronus esse videatur. ... Verum ita fere fit, ut in conflictu cum adversariis Scripturam Sacram ad suam quisque causam detorqueat"; cf. LB 6.242D.

[117] Allen 3.335ff. for Jerome's advantages over Augustine; for the awe-inspiring nature of Augustine cf. Allen 8.153: "At hic incomparabilis doctor ... ingenii plusquam *aquilinam aciem* ad necessariae veritatis investigationem intendit; ita subtilis in disputando, si res postulet acumen dialecticum, ut semper dimittat lectorem, non tantum eruditiorem verum etiam ad bene vivendum inflammatiorem. Quid enim aliud potest *ignis*, ubicunque ponas, quam urere? Amabat *vehementer* quod docebat, docebat argute quod amabat; utrunque gignit in eo qui scriptis illius propius intendit animum"; Allen 7.124: "Sed hic [Ambrosius] grandem illum *cetum* in ecclesiae sagenam petraxit, Augustinum" (my italics).

[118] Allen 3.333ff., 438ff., 4.338, 6.147, 165, 7.397f., 9.155.

stand and describe such individuals since the disentanglement of their complexities depended upon the comprehension of the innate focal point. In both Luther and Augustine Erasmus failed to pinpoint such a center of individuality. Every student of history will admit that the very nature of both characters made comprehension immensely hard to attain, but there were also additional difficulties that lay in Erasmus rather than the objects of inquiry.

Erasmus was unusually alert to the idea that historical judgments presented the subjective views of the observer rather than objective facts. This thought finds typical expression in a letter to bishop Longlond dated autum 1528 when Erasmus was working on Froben's *Augustine*. Moringus had already turned down his proposal to write a biography and thus the task of supplying a suitable introduction rested with Erasmus himself. Plausibly, the question of the Augustine biography in the back of his mind was indirectly answered when he replied to Longlond's accusation of untimely stubborness:

> As to the example of Augustine which Your Reverence admonishes me to follow: I am all the time doing just this and on my own initiative, as I delete or amend whenever I come upon something [in my writings] that needs correction. On the other hand, even after his retractations Augustine retained much that ought to be termed simply heretical if anyone today dared face the fact. Moreover the judgments of mortals vary so much that you will hardly find three who are of the same opinion.... What, I beseech you, within the reach of human affairs is really lasting? There was a time without theological schools when Augustine was considered an invincible dialectician because he had read the categories of Aristotle. But finally theology reached, —I would almost say: outreached—, the climax. ... [119]

The quotation illustrates Erasmus' precept that value judgments are subject to historical change. It also helps us to understand why, in the case of Augustine as in many others, Erasmus saw fit to point out some of their characteristics in various contexts but was never able to write a proper biography, for a biography was bound to bring into the open conflicting aspects which he could not reconcile. Moreover, the quotation reflects Erasmus' doubts about the purpose of his own recantations which, of course, was in keeping with their very limited extent. Erasmus respected within himself a static center of his personality which was incompatible with recantations; yet it was a subtle, ineffable center, and Erasmus could not tolerate that any label of the common kind be stuck to it. *"Ego nec Reuchlinista sum nec ullius humanae factionis"*, he kept repeating. [120] Erasmus was egocentric both in a literal sense and in the way that he judged everything and every character in relation to his own person. His self-respect

---

[119] Allen 7.460, 464; cf. 8.343, 9.159.
[120] Allen 4.121; cf. above n. 109.

compelled him to respect in others as well a nature that was beyond the reach of commonplace labels. The latter might be used to describe a single quality as Erasmus often did in analyzing the individual style of the classics and Church fathers, but no amalgam of commonplaces could capture the whole character of an individual. *Individuum est ineffabile:* though of unknown origin and never used in the 16th century, the expression renders the experience of Erasmus as accurately as it approximates the conclusions of Plato, Aristotle, and Thomas Aquinas.

As did other Christian humanists, Erasmus realized that the individual was governed by his own inner logic which could best be recognized against the varying background of the exterior historical circumstances. It was obviously on this basis that a good biographer would have to develop his characters. But how well could this job be accomplished? In a letter to Erasmus Thomas More expressed a very positive view, when adding his own praise for Vives' *Declamationes Syllanae* to that of Erasmus:

> I cannot sufficiently admire those merits of his *Declamations* which you have recognized so accurately and explained so appropriately. Most of all—and this is what matters most of all in declamation—he [Vives] seems to recall the history of those [distant] times so readily and completely as not everybody might remember the circumstances of his own life. And not alone this, he embraces the mental frames of people who met their fate so many centuries ago as if they were presently alive. One gets the impression that the plot of his *Declamations* has not been extracted from books; rather that he saw and sensed it and participated in the happy and unhappy events. And finally he would seem to mete out advice, not as aloof and from a distant viewpoint, but fervently and as emanating from his own fear and hope, danger and happiness. This alone would be worthy of admiration that he manages in so many cases to take one side as well as the other; but he even conducts himself in either role in such manner that you could call him a chameleon for changing his colour as well, as he turns from one to another. [121]

More's reference to the chameleon aptly points out those versatile qualities which Erasmus too found necessary for the understanding of history. He knew and disliked that oscillating property of history which required in the observer a chameleonic approach. [122] What puzzled him, however, was that the historical characters themselves looked often like chameleons. However the observer might twist himself around, he would still not gain a definitive view.

More's praise for Vives took its clue from a letter of Erasmus, published together with the *Declamationes Syllanae*. Erasmus too admired the individualizing quality of Vives' literary creation, but he did not express it in historical perspective: Vives "is involved in a fictitious argument, but in such a manner that you think he was treating a serious event. He takes

---

[121] Allen 4.267.
[122] See above pp. 19, 23f., 26 n. 64.

up either part, but so plausibly that you would think he has persuaded himself in the first place of what he is going to advise". [123]

When, on the other hand, Erasmus employed historical perspective, he often did so in a negative way. His purpose was not so much to assess the specific merits of historical figures in terms of their contributions to their epochs as to excuse their shortcomings in view of the limitations imposed by a more primitive age. Of all the authors whom he consulted frequently none made Erasmus more aware of historical change than Thomas Aquinas, the schoolman *par excellence*. When a critic took exception probably to a note in his *Novum Testamentum* where Aquinas was called a *vir indignus*, Erasmus tried unsuccessfully to appease the man by explaining:

> ... in some place I excused an error of Thomas, adding that he is an unworthy man who happened to live in those times, meaning, of course, and even expressing that Thomas would have been worthy of a happier century, for he was lacking neither intelligence nor diligence. [124]

A passage like this suggests that Thomas was a child of his times. Yet it also suggests that there are timeless human values: the same Thomas, somehow, was too good for his times. Erasmus' self-centered individual, though conditioned by time and environment, still is the receptacle of time-less and topical virtues and vices. Because that which is truly individual possessed a commonplace character, the collections of apothegms expressed for the sake of posterity the true essence of historical individuality. In 1531 the epistle dedicatory to his *Apophthegmata* stated that in such sayings, "as in an unerring mirror, there is represented the mind of individuals" and that "just as individual men have each their own character, so have individual nations". [125]

Where, as in the case of Luther, the essential character of the individual remained obscure, traditional religious percepts enabled a topical under-standing to be expressed in the assigning of a role. In this approach, emphasis passed from the unknowable intentions of the individual to the intentions of God or the devil which were *a priori* known to the Christian, even though perhaps unrecognizable in the specific event. Unlike Dante,

---

[123] Allen 4.208f.

[124] Allen 4.315f.; cf. 4.464; for Erasmus' apologetic, but basically critical approach to the achievements of past ages see Allen 4.417f., 5.192.

[125] Allen 9.126f.: "Restat historia, quae quoniam res praeclare secusve gestas velut in tabula spectandas repraesentat, nec id absque voluptate, magnatibus viris aptior esse videtur: sed hic ut infinitam voluminum vim Principi vacet evolvere, qui possit meminisse? ... Is demum occupatissimo Principi gratum praestat officium, qui aurum purum fac-tumque exhibet, qui selectas ac repurgatas gemmas auro inclusas aut poculis additas offert. Id officium quum a multis tentatum sit, mea tamen sententia, nemo felicius praestitit quam Plutarchus, qui post aeditum egregie frugiferum opus, De vitis virorum illustrium, ... Traiano Caesarum laudatissimo collegit insignia diversorum Apophthegmata, quod in his velut in certissimo speculo repraesentatur animus singulorum. ... Habent enim Apophthegmata peculiarem quandam rationem et indolem suam, ut breviter, argute, salse et urbane cuiusque ingenium exprimant. Siquidem ut singulis hominibus, ita singulis etiam nationibus suus quidam genius est...".

82

Erasmus had no special inspiration to tell him how divine providence had judged the individual characters of history. Plainly visible acts of conformity with or disregard for the divine will, however, he considered as the vital criteria for the evaluation of a man's life and place in history. Man, in the full possession of his individuality based upon Free Will, was still bound by faith to conform himself to Christ, the super-man and super-individual. No satisfactory understanding of Erasmus' view on individuality can be gained, unless one realizes that both his criteria for the apprehension of individuals and the special problems he encountered in the process were reflected and confirmed by his meditation upon Christ.

Erasmus' statements can more easily be evaluated, if one considers Cassirer's analysis of some of Cusanus' thoughts in relation to the problem of individuality. After pointing out how for Cusanus the cosmos, both physical and spiritual, is equally near and far from God, Cassirer continues :

> This thought reaches even further. It proceeds from the particularization we find in nature and in the historical forms of the intellect, all the way to the last particular, to the simply individual. From the religious viewpoint, the individual is not the opposite of the universal, but rather its true fulfilment. [126]

Cassirer then proceeds to summarize the opening passages of Cusanus' *De visione Dei*. Cusanus recalls a self-portrait of Rogier van der Weyden which seemed to fix its glance upon the spectator from whatever angle the latter was watching. We may follow Cassirer's summary of Cusanus' argument:

> This represents for us, in a sensible parable, the nature of the basic relationship between God, the all-encompassing being, and the being of the finite, the ultimate particular. Each particular and individual being has an immediate relationship to God; it stands, as it were, face to face with Him. ... So I see, oh Lord, that your face precedes every visible face, that it is the truth and the model of all faces. Therefore, any face that looks into yours sees nothing different from itself, because it sees its own truth. When I look at this picture from the east, it seems to me that I am not looking at it but it at me; the same is true when I look at it from the south or the west. Likewise, your face is turned to all who look at you. Whoever looks at you with love feels you looking lovingly at him—and the more he tries to look upon you with love, the more lovingly does your face look back at him. Whoever looks at it in anger finds your look angry; whoever looks at you joyfully finds you joyful. For as everything appears red to the physical eye when it looks through a red glass, so the spiritual eye, in its limitedness, sees you, the goal and object of the mind's observation, according to the nature of its own limitation. Man is capable only of human judgment. ... If the lion attributed a face to you, he would attribute that of a lion, the ox that of an ox, and the eagle that of an eagle. ... In all faces the face of faces appears,

---

[126] E .Cassirer, *The Individual and the Cosmos in Renaissance Philosophy*, transl. M. Domandi, New York 1964 (Harper Torchbooks), 31.

veiled, as in an enigma—but it cannot be seen uncovered unless it be when we go beyond all faces to the secret, dark silence, wherein nothing remains of the knowledge and the concept of face. [127]

Face to face with the Absolute, man must turn to Christ as the only bridge between God and man's own limitations; in Cassirer's analysis of Cusanus' thought:

> The consciousness of difference implies the meditation of difference. But this meditation cannot, in turn, mean that the infinite, the absolute being stands in some relation to the finite, empirical consciousness of self—we still cannot jump over that abyss. In place of the empirical there must be a general self; in place of the human being as an individual, particular existence, there must be the spiritual content of all humanity. This spiritual, universal content of humanity Cusanus sees in Christ. [128]

To quote finally from Cusanus' *De docta ignorantia*:

> While we journey here below the truth of our faith can subsist or continue to be only in the spirit of Christ, while the order of believers remains a high diversity in agreement, in one and the same Christ. And when we sink out of the church militant at death, we shall afterwards rise only by the power of Christ so that the church triumphant shall also be one,... so that there shall be but one humanity in all, the humanity of Christ, and one spirit, that of Christ, in all spirits, and that each may dwell in him in such a fashion that there is but one Christ in all (*unus Christus ex omnibus*). ... [129]

The thought of Cusanus elucidates that of Erasmus, although a direct influence seems improbable and their common roots in the *Devotio moderna* must remain a rather incalculable factor in such matters. Erasmus' far less philosophical diction attests to his basic debt to a much older Christian tradition which is in essence Pauline.

In Christ Erasmus sees the "archetype", [130] at once the supreme topical example and the sublimation of individuality. Christ is the "head" of the

---

[127] Ibid. 31-33; N. Cusanus, *Opera*, Paris 1514 (Frankfurt a.M. 1962), 1.99-101; cf. Erasmus' expression, LB 1.852E: "At Deus unico intuitu contuetur universa, praesentia, praeterita et futura...".

[128] E. Cassirer, *The Individual* 39.

[129] N. Cusanus, *De docta ignorantia* 3.12 (ed. E. Hoffmann and R. Klibansky, Leipzig 1932, 158f.): "Quapropter veritas fidei nostrae, dum hic peregrinamur, non potest nisi in spiritu Christi subsistere, remanente ordine credentium, ut sit diversitas in concordantia in uno Iesu. Et dum absolvimur ex hac militanti ecclesia, quando resurgemus, non aliter quam in Christo resurgere poterimus, ut sic etiam sit una triumphantium ecclesia, et quisque in ordine suo. Et tunc veritas carnis nostrae non erit in se, sed in veritate carnis Christi, et veritas corporis nostri in veritate corporis Christi, et veritas spiritus nostri in veritate spiritus Christi Iesu, ut palmites in vite, ut sit una Christi humanitas in omnibus hominibus, et unus Christi spiritus in omnibus spiritibus; ita ut quodlibet in eo sit, ut sit unus Christus ex omnibus. Et tunc qui unum ex omnibus qui Christi sunt, in hac vita recipit, Christum recipit." The translation quoted is by G. Heron (London 1954, 167); cf. E. Cassirer, *The Individual* 70f.

[130] E.g. LB 5.32A, 39B, 142D, 6.713F.

84

mystical body of Christendom. [131] He must lower himself to the lesser members of that body, assuming responsibility for their "individual" weaknesses and sins. [132] The members, in turn, bear the indelible mark of their common dependence upon the head: in Christ they are all one and the superficial differences of rank and race must fade. [133] Many of Erasmus' formulations are visibly indebted to the letters of Paul.

In *Ratio verae theologiae* Erasmus introduces another image which derives from early Christian thought. Christ is the center of three concentric circles with different radii. Representing the three estates of clergy, nobility, and common people, the three circles form the universe of Christendom. [134] Similarly, Christian doctrine is a circle based upon the individual life of Christ:

> In the books of Plato and Seneca you might perhaps find [precepts] that do not offend the tenets of Christ; in the life of Socrates you will find

---

[131] E.g. LB 5.31A, 45D, 1357F; cf. *Romans* 12.4-5, 1. *Corinthians* 12.12, *Ephesians* 1.22-23.

[132] LB 5.85F-86A: "Et quoniam totus ferme Christi sermo figuris ac tropis obliquus est, diligenter odorabitur theologiae candidatus, quam sustineat personam is qui loquitur, capitis an membrorum, pastoris an gregis. Siquidem Christus cum in cruce Patrem inclamans ait: *Deus meus, Deus meus, cur deseruisti me?*..., non capitis, sed membrorum suorum voce loquitur, auctore divo Augustino. Item dum moeret, dum angitur, dum poculum deprecatur, dum rursus, quasi corrigens quod dixerat, suae voluntati renunciat, Patris voluntati sese submittit, videtur membrorum affectum in se transtulisse"; LB 5.1056F-1057A: "Adhaec quoniam Christus et corpus ipsius mysticum idem sunt, Dominus quaedam in se recipit, quae non in ipsum, sed in illius membra competunt. Veluti quod ex Psalmo XXI Christus in cruce pendens usurpat: *Longe a salute mea verba delictorum meorum*, ad Christi corpus pertinet, cuius peccata in se recepit...: quae omnia a membris transferuntur in caput, eo quod caput et corpus unum sunt, quemadmodum maritus et uxor una caro sunt, quod mysterium Paulus appellat magnum in Christo sponso et Ecclesia sponsa. Agnoscit hanc individuam societatem etiam sensus communis et vulgaris loquendi consuetudo: si quis laedat pedem aut aliud membrum, lingua clamat: cur me laedis?...".

[133] LB 4.632D: "Quid autem tam idem esse potest quam eiusdem corporis membra? Ab hoc igitur neque servus est quisquam, neque liber, neque Barbarus, neque Graecus, neque vir, neque foemina, sed omnes idem in Christo sunt, qui omnia redigit in concordiam" (cf. below n. 137); LB 5.27C: "Perfectum erit, si dissolvi cupiant et esse cum Christo, si in morbis, damnis reliquisque fortunae incommodis gloriam et gaudium suum constituant, quod digni habeantur, qui vel hoc modo Capiti suo conformentur"; LB 5.41D: "Illi sibi placeant quod in aulis principum versentur; tu elige cum David abiectus esse in domo Dei. Attende quos elegerit Christus, infirmos, stultos, ignobiles secundum mundum. In Adam omnes ignobiles nascimur, in Christo omnes unum sumus. Vera nobilitas est... servum esse Christi."

[134] LB 5.88C-E: "...non abs re fuerit, universum Christi populum in tres circulos dividere, quorum omnium tamen unicum sit centrum, Christus Jesus, ad cuius simplicissimam puritatem pro sua cuique virile enitendum est omnibus. ... Tertium circulum promiscuo vulgo dare licebit, ceu crassissimae huius orbis quem fingimus parti, sed ita crassissimae ut nihilo secius ad Christi corpus pertineat, quanquam in singulis circulis ordinem aliquem imaginari licet...."; the same concept was expressed much earlier in Allen 3.368; Erasmus' argument rests firmly on early Christian views as summarized by O. Cullmann, *Christ and Time* 187f.: "Church and world are ... two concentric circles, whose common center is Christ. ... The inner surface stands in closer relation to Christ than does the outer one, and yet Christ is the common center. Thus the alternative between two areas and one area does not exist in the New Testament. The relation is more complex. This will become clear especially in the Primitive Christian attitude to the State"; cf. N. Cusanus, *De docta ignorantia* ch. 23: God is like an infinite sphere whose center may be equated with its surface.

[aspects] that are in complete agreement with the life of Christ, but that circle and a harmony that brings all matters into common agreement you will find in Christ alone. In the Prophets many a divinely inspired dictum is to be found and many a pious deed; and many there are in Moses and other men renowned for their saintly lives. But that circle you will find in no man, that circle which started out from the Prophets and completed its circuit in the life and doctrines of the Apostles and martyrs. [135]

Erasmus continues his argument in *Ratio verae theologiae* by showing "how Christ adjusted himself to those whom he wanted to pull over to himself"; [136] hence he had to accept the idiosyncrasies of so many individuals, sinner and saint, fisherman and publican, Jew and pagan. No wonder that with all this variety in his life and message he would finally look like a "Proteus". This variety does not disrupt the essential harmony of Christ; rather it enhances harmony as do the artful arrangements of polyphonous music. *"Sic omnia factus est omnibus, ut nusquam tamen sui dissimilis esset."* [137]

Is this not again that central, universal Lord who, with the image of Cusanus, looks simultaneously every individual straight in the eye and reduces individualities to unity by making *unum Christum ex omnibus?*

Still, to follow again Erasmus' *Ratio verae theologiae*, there remain the obvious difficulties in harmonizing the apparent inconsistencies in Christ's life and teaching. At times he displays the hall-marks of his divine nature, but then again he conceals his divinity and labours and suffers like a man; at times he answers a question evasively by a counter-question. [138] But with all this, Christ is still the archetype, the "mould" (*forma*) to which the life and message of the Apostles respond. Paul, above all, resembles his master by adjusting himself to various groups and individuals: "with how much cunning (*vafricie*) did not Paul play the chameleon, if I may say so, ... so that from all directions he might bring some gain to Christ?" [139] In one of his letters Erasmus repeats in the Apostle's own language: "thus Paul

---

[135] LB 5.91F-92C.

[136] LB 5.92-98, in particular 97F, 94B: "Adeo cum nostro Christo nihil sit simplicius, tamen arcano quodam consilio Proteum quemdam repraesentat varietate vitae atque doctrinae."

[137] LB 5.92E; cf. Allen 5.185: "Sic enim obscurati, vere fuerimus gloriosi si nos ex nobis nihil essemus, sed Christus esset omnia in omnibus"; cf. *Colossians* 3.11: "Ubi non est Gentilis et Judaeus, circumcisio et praeputium, Barbarus et Scytha, servus et liber: sed omnia et in omnibus Christus."

[138] LB 5.92E, 93EF, 94CD.

[139] LB 5.98F; the use of the term *chameleon* without disparaging connotations is quite rare both in the work of Erasmus and of other humanists. More who used the expression approvingly (see above p. 81) may have owed it to J. Pico's *Oratio de hominis dignitate* ("... Et si [homo] nulla creaturarum sorte contentus, in *unitatis centrum suae* se receperit, unus cum Deo spiritus factus, in solitaria Patris caligine, qui est super omnia constitutus, omnibus antestabit. Quis hunc nostrum *chamaeleonta* non admiretur? Aut omnino quis aliud quidquam admiretur magis? Quem non immerito Asclepius Atheniensis, versipellis huius et seipsam transformantis naturae argumento, per *Proteum* in mysteriis significari dixit.) Erasmus' use of the term *chameleon* too may signal one of his many debts to the Platonic tradition. However, his ultimate purpose is the imitation of Christ rather than the glorification of man.

becomes all things to all men, so he might win them all to Christ". [140] Augustine too exhibited in his letters a versatility that called for the same Pauline terminology. [141]

That the individual should imitate Christ to the best of his abilities, is the basic precept of Erasmus' *philosophia Christi*; however, the better an individual succeeds in imitating Christ's protean universality, the more that individual's self becomes undefinable. In Christ one thus finds the proto-types of the difficulties that baffled the biographer Erasmus. Erasmus came to reject professional historiography and biography, because they did not solve—and often did not even tackle—the problems that seemed vital to him, the problems encountered in the meditation of Christ.

Christ, the "Silenus", is hiding beneath the "figures and tropes" of the Bible. From the Old Testament he speaks to mankind "*sub personas*", and still in the New Testament confusion may arise from not noticing in whose name a word is spoken. [142] One recalls that personal names were for Erasmus an important criterion in the evaluation of characters. And now he notes that the Bible has more different names for the Son than for the Father, while even the Father's "ineffable nature" calls for quite a variety of names. [143] Although Christ's nature and message are everlasting and unchangeable, he himself had found it necessary, Erasmus believed, to con-front the dumbness of his first disciples by revealing himself but gradually, progressing from ordinary humanity to the super-humanity of prophets and the divinity confirmed by his resurrection. [144]

In this way Christ was deliberately "playing roles (*personam induit*").[145] Paul followed the Lord's example when acting various roles to suit his varying audiences; while ordinary mortals had normally but one role. Whereas in the case of the God-Man as in the case of many mortals the individual is beyond human comprehension, some *roles,* at least, can be indicated. The objective, fact-finding truth of which historians and bio-graphers often boast is exceedingly hard to achieve; in the case of Christ it is simply impossible. However, the subjective relation between the self and the other individual may be within the grasp of human understanding. The more the individual Luther proved undefinable in any objective way, the more Erasmus turned to the assessment of Luther's role in relation to him-self, to Christian humanism and to the whole epoch. The more the Christian humanists realized that an objective comprehension of divinity as attempted by scholasticism, was impossible, the more they emphasized the subjective relation between the individual self and Christ. Christ became "everything

---

140 Allen 4.488: "Sic Paulus omnia fit omnibus, ut omnes Christo lucrifaciat"; cf. 1. *Corinthians* 9.22: "Factus sum infirmis infirmus, ut infirmos lucrifacerem. Omnibus omnia factus sum, ut omnes facerem salvos."

141 See Appendix, lines 28ff.

142 Cf. above n. 132; LB 2.771D, 5.207A-D, 1056C-E.

143 LB 5.1088B, 1090D.

144 LB 5.1092f. especially 1093DE.

145 LB 5.1056D.

to everybody"; Erasmus, like Cusanus, saw in him the bridge that gulfed the abyss between the Absolute and the individual. The *Enchiridion militis Christiani* and the *Praeparatio ad mortem* offer perhaps the clearest expression of how much Erasmus valued a personalized, undogmatic relation between the individual member and Christ, the head; [146] an esteem which he shared not only with the late-medieval mystics but also with many radicals of the Reformation.

The mortal individual could approach Christ more easily because Christ had first approached him. Although his christology may primarily emphasize the mystery of the *logos,* Erasmus did not ignore Christ's human individuality. Repeatedly he described how Christ in order to redeem mankind had first to accept the inadequacies of the human condition. [147] *Christ,* the very name, refers to that human condition. [148] In his first theological treatise, a *disputatiuncula* with Colet on Christ's agony in the garden of Gethsemane, Erasmus maintained that Christ, in his human nature, felt fear and terror as he looked ahead to his death on the cross. [149] All his life Erasmus reiterated the same view. [150] Moreover, it was not only the human Christ whom Erasmus contemplated in a most unheroic pose: the symbolic Christ, as envisaged in the mystery of Silenus and similar sights of outward foolishness, was equally unheroic.

The foolish and fearful human Christ was one pole, and Erasmus' equally unheroic self-consciousness was another pole around which there rotated a comprehensive vision of weak, unglorified humanity. At times it is hard to harmonize this vision with the humanistic assertion of Free Will and the positive potential of human dignity. As Paul Huber has rightly emphasized, a similar individualizing and unheroic view of mankind can be found in Thomas More. [151] The message of Christian humanism differs here manifestly from the unfettered, heroic individualism of Italian humanism which persistently indulged in the creation of Promethean imagery. Erasmus, for one, had little use for heaven-storming, God-defying Prometheus. [152]

---

[146] LB 5.25A, 30F-31A, 54F-55A: "... cogita, o membrum infimum, quantus sit Christus caput tuum..."; LB 5.142C-E, 1296E: "Ille natus est puer, sed quod non omisit Esaias: nobis natus est, nobis datus est. Itidem nobis docuit, nobis sanavit morbos...".

[147] LB 5.1271BC: "At minime convenit illi perfectam hominis naturam tribuere et id detrahere, quo nihil est cum natura coniunctius. Quod si utrumque iuxta naturale est, ut anima et praesenti malo doleat et de imminente affligatur, cur non utrumque homini Christo aut relinquimus aut adimimus? Imo dabo unde liqueat ei fuisse causam, cur mortem expavesceret non tantum ut homines caeteri, verum etiam acrius quam quisquam hominum"; it should be noticed how often Erasmus was compelled to defend his view in his apologetic writings: e.g. Allen 3.328, LB 9.32-36, 571DE.

[148] LB 5.207A.

[149] LB 5.1265ff., Allen 1.245ff.

[150] Cf. the passage from *Ratio verae theologiae* (1518) quoted in n. 132 and a similar one in the *Praeparatio ad mortem* (1534): LB 5.1300D.

[151] P. Huber, *Traditionsfestigkeit und Traditionskritik bei Thomas Morus,* Basel 1953, see the sections on "das individuelle Erleben" (157ff.) and "das unheroische Menschenbild" (161ff.).

[152] In Erasmus' youthful story of Cain's theft of wheat from Paradise, Cain bears some Promethean features, but not those of tragic dignity and glory (Allen 1.269f.). I know of only one serious reference to Prometheus: LB 5.787E.

The individual, though ever-present, is by no means supreme in the cosmos of Christian humanism. One recalls how in More's view Henry VIII insisted unduly upon the rights of the individual, whereas More himself in opposing the King's will was not guilty of individual disobedience, but merely conformed himself to the overruling consensus of the body of Christendom. With regard to this same consensus, neither More nor Erasmus would accord an unqualified supremacy to the Popes who were, after all, individuals. [153]

Erasmus' unheroic and confusingly complex view of individuality is important because of the prominent place which individual personalities occupied in his view of history. [154] There can be no doubt that had Erasmus ever been inclined to write universal history, that history would have focused upon such pillars as the Church fathers and such *Sileni* as Socrates and Cato, St. Paul and St. Francis, all of whom were the true heirs of Christ's individualism. But not before the Reformation had planted a new heroic ideal of martyrdom and a new appreciation of heroism would that sort of historical approach fully materialize. In the Reformation, however, it flourished with such un-Erasmian products as John Foxe's *Book of Martyrs* as well as with the eminently Erasmian and Erasmus-inspired work of Sebastian Franck.

VI

Real history for Erasmus was history sub *specie aeternitatis*; historical meditation in the truest sense was meditation of the Scriptures. In this light Erasmus' patristic editions and his own Scriptural commentaries could be considered his personal contribution to the study of history. The biographer Erasmus must be approached in the same way and the peculiar nature of his biographical sketches should corroborate our findings with regard to his view of history. In examining Erasmus' biographies one must bear in mind that for all his skilful painting of individual features and shades of features his ultimate goal was to show the individual character *sub specie aeternitatis,* as a lasting typus and example. What finally mattered was the degree of participation in and the peculiar contribution of an individual to the dialogue of Christ with his flock. This dialogue between Christ and his saints, in which basic disagreement was unthinkable, formulated the

---

[153] P. Huber, *Traditionsfestigkeit* 132ff.; R. Padberg, *Erasmus als Katechet* 103f. Cf. LB 5.89BC: "Atque haud scio an pontifices, etiamsi maxime velint, possint ita moderari leges suas... ut per omnia Christi decretis respondeant. Christus ... praecepit ea quae coelum sapiant. Pontifices homines et hominibus infirmis—atque adeo varie infirmis—pro tempore praescribunt, quod videtur expedire. Proinde fieri non potest, quin in horum quoque placitis interdum insint quaedam, quae sapiant humanos affectus..."
[154] See above p. 35f.

consensus of the Church. In *Praeparatio ad mortem* Erasmus considered the lasting truth of the Scriptural canon:

> If God were to speak to you through some created species, in view of the example of certain pious men you might perhaps be somewhat hesitant, lest some subterfuge might come into the picture (*numquid fuci lateret in imagine*). But from such hesitation we all have been exempted by the everlasting consensus of the Catholic church. [155]

Who were the pious individuals whose example might confuse those in search of the truth? Perhaps men like Augustine and Luther whose individuality could not well be pinned down and whose lasting image was accordingly hard to assess? However that may be, the assurance of truth resulted from the consensus, and what finally counted with regard to the individual was his individual contribution to the consensus. It was in this sense that biography attracted Erasmus.

In his youth Erasmus had painted [156] and, pen in hand, he remained an admirable painter for all his life. The comparison between pictorial and rhetorical expression runs through the entire argument of the *Ciceronianus* and shows him well aware of the visualizing capacity of the written word. Both in his scattered references to historical characters—St. Francis may be recalled—and in his more substantial biographical portraits he followed the maxim which he had placed at the beginning of his description of Thomas More: ἐκ τοῦ ὁρᾶν γίγνεται ἀνθρώποις τ'ἐρᾶν. Erasmus' ambition was to make the individual visible in his living and lasting qualities rather than through the story of his life. Projection into the temporal space of a *curriculum vitae* was a means which he used but sparingly. Moreover, he could not attempt a portrayal unless he knew himself in sympathy with the character to be depicted.

W. Rüegg has shown that this sort of visual presentation stemmed from Erasmus' adherence to the ideals of Ciceronian humanism. Ciceronian humanism endeavoured to involve the reader personally in the presented argument. This was best achieved in the literary form of the dialogue. [157] Erasmus skilfully created an atmosphere of dialogue by presenting his biographies either as personal letters intended for a wide circulation or as prefaces to his great patristic editions where the reader should meet the author before attending to his literary compositions. Even "Moria" begins her *encomium* with an autobiographical sketch. Before appraising her own work, she introduces herself to the audience by using such traditional *topoi* of identification as name, descent, place of birth, and upbringing. [158]

In 1516 Froben published his great edition of Jerome which was directed by Erasmus and accompanied by Erasmus' fullest and most remark-

---

[155] LB 5.1296F-1297A.
[156] Allen 1.91n.
[157] W. Rüegg, *Cicero und der Humanismus* 86, 123 and passim.
[158] LB 4.408-411.

able biography. *Eximii Doctoris Hieronymi Stridonensis vita ex ipsius potissimum litteris contexta* has been carefully edited by W. K. Ferguson whose introduction and commentary make it unnecessary to re-examine the work at great length. The Jerome edition reflects Erasmus' life-long interest and unsurpassed love for this father and represents well over a decade of intermittent scholarly work. Significantly, this labour of love had gone hand in hand with preparation of Erasmus' *New Testament,* and both editions were finally to appear in the same year. If the Bible was the primary source for Erasmus' *storia ideal eterna,* the works of Jerome, the great translator and commentator of the Bible, would ideally complement Erasmus' own contribution to history. Erasmus left the reader in no doubt that both with the Jerome edition and the accompanying biography he intended to set forth a model of philological and historical veracity.

Moreover, the life of Jerome, the second glory of Bethlehem and the first explorer of *philosophia Christi* ("*Bethlehem bis felicissima, et quod in hac Christus natus sit mundo, et quod in eadem Hieronymus natus sit coelo— ex evangelicis et apostolicis litteris, velut ex purissimis fontibus, Christi philosophiam hauriebat*"), [159] provided a personal link between Christ and Erasmus himself. In the light of this, one understands Erasmus' willingness to provide Jerome, of all people, with a biography.

The biography opens with a remarkable introduction (lines 1-78) which repeats Erasmus' usual criticism of the "*fabulamenta*" of traditional historiography as represented by Herodotus and others. Strangely enough this criticism is part of a bold argument in favour of historical truth. Truth is said "to have its own face which no make-up can imitate" and "its own energy which no artifice can equal". The use of fictitious stories is not permissible, even though they might serve a moral and pious purpose, as was the case "when in the days of old far-sighted men glorified with fabulous miracles whatever they wished to urge upon the crowd, such as the worship of the gods, the origin of cities and races, the beginning of noble families...".

Not so much this rationalism as such, pregnant though it is with the attitudes of the future, but its application to history is unique in the work of Erasmus. The logical conclusion would seem to be that, for once at least, Erasmus positively envisaged a historical science and proceeded to demonstrate its methods in the life of Jerome. Yet if this biography is a historical essay of singular vigour and value, one must say that Erasmus never again availed himself of the model here created. In part, this failure is accounted for by circumstantial reasons which would not apply to anyone but Jerome. Erasmus' intimate knowledge of and special veneration for Jerome's work called for a vindication of the Saint in the face of medieval and incompetent biographers as well as such unsympathetic ones as Rufinus whom Erasmus thought chronically negligent of his duties as a translator and historian alike. [160]

---

159 *Hieronymi vita* 1559ff., 492f.
160 *Hieronymi vita* 8-12; Allen 7.103.

After a forceful critique of the sources (79-135), Erasmus gives a detailed biography from birth to death, weaving into the roughly chronological outline such topics as family and personal contacts, journeys and sojourns, education and scholarship, spiritual progress and fame (136-1020). The second part of the essay is less homogeneous. It starts with virtual appendices to the *vita* which state Erasmus' opinion on the controversial issues of Jerome's virginity and the merits of his literary style, his famous vision and his theology (1021-1229). This section is perhaps the boldest and most valuable one. There follow finally the judgments on Jerome by contemporaries and posterity, interspersed with Erasmus' own conclusions gained in part by comparison with other fathers (1230-1565).

Otherwise, the *Hieronymi vita* shows again that Erasmus did not view a man's life as a sequence of phases dominated by different interests and divided by crises or sudden revelations. He mentioned Jerome's baptism (265ff.) and his experiments with asceticism (397ff.) as the natural stages of a uniform development. Whereas Jerome himself remorsefully remembered the classics that he had taken with him to his desert seclusion, Erasmus flatly ignored the incompatibility of the scholarly and ascetic ideals: "*hic annos quatuor ab hominum frequentia semotus, cum solo Christo cumque libris habebat commercium*" (473f.). In the same breath, Erasmus spoke of Jerome's "zealous wish to wash off in a rain of tears the lapses of his youth". This is the first time that such youthful sins were mentioned. Only Jerome's famous "dream" or "vision" was judged sufficiently important to warrant a hint about the changing attitude of Jerome himself: the critics "may look for themselves whether they prefer believing the old man or the adolescent. That it was no dream, the youthful lad wrote; that it was a dream, the aged man wrote (1152-54)".

Between 1519 and 1521 Erasmus composed the literary portraits of three personal friends: Thomas More, John Colet, and Jean Vitrier. All were meticulously executed character portraits, and yet the artist felt urged to express some dissatisfaction with his work. The portraits form the substance of two letters to personal friends and were, according to Erasmus, written upon request. No such requests have been preserved for us. In any case it is clear that he wrote for the general public as well and wished to impress upon his readers an air of circumstance rather than deliberate tooling. In *Hieronymi vita* he had written history; here he insisted that he was painting. The fact-establishing features of a *curriculum vitae* are scarce and of very subordinate nature. The *vita* of Jean Vitrier, in particular, might be labelled the portrait of an unknown friar: whereas Erasmus called forth a character sparkling with individuality, historians still cannot reproduce the most elementary data of the friar's life.

The first to pose for Erasmus, and the only still living at the time, was Thomas More, whose biography can be found in a letter to Hutten dated from July 1519. [161] In the affairs of no other man had Erasmus ever taken

---

[161] Allen 4.12ff.

a similar interest, and the famous text is therefore an unique tribute to Eramus' best friend. Yet to its author it was far from definitive. In two more letters he later attended to comparable, though less homogeneous, descriptions of More's character and environment. [162] Of these later letters the first one, addressed to Budé and written just after the descriptions of Vitrier and Colet, must be mentioned here as it complements the letter to Hutten in two important aspects.

In the letter to Hutten Erasmus' first and last thought expressed the difficulties of the attempted essay. More was a man with many varied gifts, among them a mind perpetually active, engaged to think ahead of others ("*ingenium praesens et ubique praevolans*"). [163] The subsequent letter to Budé emphasized again More's vigorous and versatile mind combined with his charity to others, but here Erasmus used terms that recall some of his references to Christ, Paul, and Augustine: "*at Morus hoc agit ut omnibus nominibus et apud omnes bene audiat—tamen vix alium reperies qui magis sit omnibus omnium horarum homo*". [164]

The other aspect which is given broad attention in the earlier letter on More and then resumed in the later one with fresh and charming detail is Erasmus' wholehearted delight with More's family life. One feels that Erasmus here beheld a practical application of *philosophia Christi* with which his own nature was incompatible, that he admired in More not so much his own disciple as rather a congenial spirit endowed with many qualities that Erasmus himself lacked. It is on this basis that he envisaged a Plutarch-like comparison between the lives of More and Budé, but regrettably did not go beyond a mere hint.

If the *vita* of More is approached in this way, the two remaining por-traits of Vitrier and Colet will readily fall in line. Both are contained in a letter to Jodocus Jonas, dated from June 1521; [165] but, at least in Colet's case, Erasmus' intention to write a biography can be traced back to a moment very shortly after the completion of the 1519 letter on More. The latter dated from July; in October Erasmus learned of Colet's death and announced his desire to pay tribute to the dead friend, if their common acquaintances in England were willing to supply biographical material. [166] By encompassing the life of Vitrier as well, the project finally materialized in the form of another juxtaposition between two cognate characters thus exposing Plutarchian over-tones. It also follows up the basic theme of the letter on More and, perhaps, even the *Hieronymi vita*. If Jerome presented significant affinities with Erasmus' own realization of *philosophia Christi*, two more examples of other approaches were now added to that of More, the lay man: Vitrier embodied the ideals of Christian humanism under the cowl of a friar; Colet applied them to the office of a priest and prelate. Both

---

[162] Allen 4.576ff., 10.135ff.; cf. Allen's n. 4.12.
[163] Allen 4.13: "... οὐ παντὸς ἀνδρός ἐστιν omnes Mori dotes perspexisse; 4.12f.
[164] Allen 4.578.
[165] Allen 4.507ff.
[166] Allen 4.87-94.

were remarkably complete expressions of Christ's own spirit: "I must own that I never yet saw any one in whose character I did not after all miss some trait of Christian sincerity when compared with the single-mindedness of the two whom I am about to describe." [167]

Moreover, all three friends, the living one no less than the two deceased were pictured *sub specie aeternitatis* in the literal sense. Of Vitrier and Colet Erasmus stated: "and if you take my word for it, Jonas, you will not hesitate to enroll these two in the calendar of saints though no pope should ever canonize them"; of More he said: "with his friends he used to converse about the life to come in such a manner that you ought to admit that he spoke from the depth of his soul and with the fullest hope". [168]

Yet neither the literary charm nor the historical significance of these letters are adequately reflected by our attempted classification. The portraits remain unequalled expressions of Erasmus' highly developed sense of individuality. They still strike the reader as the perfect presentations of three thoroughly different characters. They do not follow a stereotype literary recipe; [169] rather each description has its peculiar structure designed according to the varying amount of biographical information available to Erasmus. [170] Each of them reveals the special and personal relation between the biographer and his object and thus expresses Erasmus' remarkable respect for the congeniality of very different characters. Of Vitrier it is said that he liked in Erasmus a "*hominem sui multum dissimilem*". [171] As Erasmus sees him, he was too much of an individualist to fit himself smoothly into the monastic way of life upon which he too had entered in youthful inexperience:

> I have repeatedly heard him say that to sleep and wake and return to sleep again by the sound of a bell, to talk and leave off talking, to come and go, to eat and desist from eating, to do everything, in short, by man's injunction instead of by the rule of Christ, was the life of idiots rather than of religious men. Nothing, he would aver, was more unreasonable than equality among men so unequal.... Yet at no time did he either counsel anyone else to change this way of life, or attempt anything of the kind himself, being ready to bear all things sooner than be a stumbling block in anyone's way. [172]

The quoted lines, together with many others, should be read with the addressee in mind as well as the writer. Allen and Olin have pointed out

---

[167] Allen 4.508, quoted from Lupton's revised translation in J.C. Olin, *Desiderius Erasmus* 165.

[168] Allen 4.21, 527 (J.C. Olin's transl.: *Desiderius Erasmus* 191).

[169] See M. Schütt, *Die englische Biographik* 31ff.; Schütt indicates some Aristotelian *topoi* in the biography of More, but emphasizes that their presence does not preclude original observation. The structural pattern which she delineates is not convincing.

[170] Cf. the difficulties Erasmus experienced in obtaining biographical data for his life of Colet: Allen's n. 4.507.

[171] Allen 4.508.

[172] Ibid.; J.C. Olin's transl.: *Desiderius Erasmus* 166f.

that this letter documents Erasmus' efforts to dissuade Jonas from openly joining the Lutherans. [173] The two lives, both truly representative of *philosophia Christi,* were presented at the moment when Erasmus had wearily decided that Luther's was not, but before he had experienced in full the embarrassing confrontation with Luther's incomprehensibility. We have already stated our opinion that the Luther dilemma must partly account for the fact that Erasmus henceforward undertook no biographical writing of comparable scope and level. However, it should also be remembered that the letter to Jonas was written just a few months before Erasmus' departure for Basel.

During the eight years Erasmus spent at Basel, an impressive succession of major patristic editions emerged from the presses [174] but none of Erasmus' prefaces showed any resemblance to a proper biography. To some degree this fact may be accounted for by circumstantial obstacles. When Erasmus edited the commentary on the Psalms by the younger of the two Arnobii, biographical information was so scant and vague that he ascribed the work to the wrong author; [175] and when prefacing the Irenaeus edition, he referred repeatedly to the fifth book of Eusebius' *historia Ecclesiastica,* but clearly was in no position to either check on or add to Eusebius' notes. [176] Nevertheless, in most cases it is hard to deny that some biographical outline was both feasible and desirable.

Ever more distinctly Erasmus felt that he was growing old. His time was now too precious for the careful biographical research which he had once lavished on Jerome. He may have been less certain of the merits of such an exercise and he was too busy with the texts to be edited. The more he realized the ineffability of individual character, the more he insisted that the great teachers of Christendom should speak for themselves. No biography could ever present them adequately: their own complete and authentic works must be made available. Typically it was in his prefaces to patristic editions that Erasmus defended his pious devotion to text criticism at the expense of his own writing. [177]

It was, nevertheless, clear to Erasmus that there existed not only a need for critical and comprehensive editions, but that the reader deserved every possible guidance in mining the precious ore that was made accessible in the thousands of folio pages covered with patristic literature. He continued to provide generous and often elaborate prefaces to the father editions. In the preface to Froben's *Ambrose* of 1527 he used copious biographical detail to demonstrate the actuality of the bishop's shining example in the troubled days of the Sack of Rome. But then he stopped abruptly,

---

[173] Allen 4.507; J.C. Olin, *Desiderius Erasmus* 164.

[174] Cyprian 1519, Arnobius 1522, Hilary 1523, Irenaeus 1526, Ambrose 1527, Augustine 1528.

[175] Cf. Allen's n. 5.99f.

[176] Allen 6.384ff.

[177] Allen 7.101, 119f.

remarking: *"sed desino, ne vitae Ambrosianae videar historiam texere"* [178] and therewith proceeded to presenting the judgments on Ambrose by other fathers and to analyzing his style in comparison with that of other fathers. Similarly in other prefaces, as he approached the critical point where a characterization of the author seemed in place, he preferred to let the fathers speak for themselves and about one another.

If Erasmus ever believed that his elaborate prefaces adequately replaced a biography he thought differently in 1528. He was anxious to solicit a biography for Froben's *Augustine,* only to be told in return that one was indeed expected—but by himself. [179] Then he could not comply, but in subsequent patristic editions he twice tried to satisfy those readers who might be looking for a biography.

To his epistle dedicatory for the Chrysostom edition of 1530 he appended a biography of about half the size of *Hieronymi vita.* It was an unenthusiastic piece of work which he himself characterized more accurately than he might have wished by calling it a *"longam ac molestam praefationis farraginem".* [180] A *farrago* it certainly was. Erasmus followed his sources, chiefly the *historia tripartita,* very closely. He also re-employed a characterization of Chrysostom in the central section of a former epistle dedicatory quite literally. [181] Faced with the dramatic developments of Chrysostom's life the biographer Erasmus was at a loss. The central figure is often obscured by numerous and poorly identified secondary figures. The essay lacks the vigorous structure of *Hieronymi vita* and affords little evidence of Erasmus' critical inquisitiveness.

In contrast, Erasmus' introductory essay *"De vita, phrase, docendi ratione et operibus Origenis",* written for the Origen edition of 1536, opens on a more promising note. Erasmus first discussed Origen's names which, once again, revealed the will of Providence and pinpointed the significance of the entire life: *"quod si magnis viris nomina non fortuito tribuuntur, sed per divinam providentiam habent futurorum praesagia, utrumque nomen mire quadrat in hunc eximium Ecclesiae doctorem".* [182] Erasmus then took up the method he had been using in *Hieronymi vita:* he concentrated on only the most significant events and developments while giving them a thorough scrutiny. In this way he proceeded as far as Origen's self-emasculation at the threshold of mature manhood, an act that Erasmus had always approached with strong feelings. But then—as if the biographer had suddenly tired—the remaining part of Origen's life is cursorily presented in less than a column. No attempt is made to assess Origen's character; and his orthodoxy, another point on which Erasmus had strong views, is not even mentioned. In the following chapter on Origen's learning, a comparison with other fathers is feebly attempted, but there is nothing to remind the

---

[178] Allen 7.123.
[179] See above p. 77f.
[180] LB 3.1347C.
[181] LB 3.1343E-1346C; Allen 6.488-490.
[182] LB 8.425AB.

96

reader of the crucial importance which the conflicting opinions of Origen and Augustine had for Erasmus. In his discussion of Origen's works Erasmus limited himself to the question of authenticity.

Why did the old Erasmus undertake these two biographies? Origen surely was the last character to suit a biographer who had firmly set his mind on avoiding controversy. In addition, Erasmus himself held conflicting views on Origen that were hard to harmonize. Although he felt sincere and uncommon admiration for both fathers, the biography of Chrysostom was too hastily done and that of Origen too non-committal to be called a labour of love. The only explanation seems that he wished to make as good as possible the two editions of beloved fathers.

This last group of biographical writings is supplemented by two short commemorative sketches of the character of Archbishop Warham written after his death and published in 1533 and 1535. [183] They present a colourless *encomium* along the lines of the medieval bishop's *vita* [184] but, at least, they further emphasize the similarities of scope in Erasmus' last biographies with the brilliant series of portraits dedicated to Jerome, More, Colet and Vitrier. Even in this thin aftercrop of his biographical writing Erasmus celebrated the common devotion to *philosophia Christi* that distinguished the Christian fathers and the Christian humanists alike.

There is some evidence of a favourable response to Erasmus' biographies from among his contemporaries. Moringus, who himself wrote several biographies, including one of Augustine, expressed his admiration for *Hieronymi vita*. [185] Allen notes an English translation, in 1533, of the letter addressed to Jonas containing the portraits of Vitrier and Colet. [186] The sketch of More, finally, did not visibly influence Roper's biography of his father-in-law since the biographer could exploit an incomparable wealth of personal recollections. But already in the subsequent life of More by Harpsfield Erasmus' letter is used as an obvious source.

Additional evidence on Erasmus' influence may be forthcoming. It seems improbable, however, that his few biographical essays should signal a major inspiration or even turning-point in the history of biography. The place of Erasmus in the development of biography is determined by the general impact of his thought and expression rather than the few biographical sketches. More important than his own biographies was no doubt his insistence on a methodical and exhaustive study of an author's works. Hand in hand with Froben he gave new lustre to the ideal of definitive *opera omnia* editions and such editions represent the major achievement of Basel's printing industry throughout the 16th century. Erasmus may also have been instrumental in gaining acceptance for the principle that no satisfactory biography of an intellectual can be written unless a good and complete

---

[183] Allen 10.146f.; LB 5.810E-812B.
[184] Cf. M. Schütt, *Die englische Biographik* 33.
[185] Allen 7.393.
[186] Allen's n. 4.507.

edition of his works was available. Erasmus' preoccupation with reliable editions was further enhanced by his often expressed view that professional historians were unreliable. His respect for the undescribable quality of an individual character confirmed his lack of confidence in the attainment of historical truth.

Despite the scant attention of contemporaries and modern scholars, Erasmus' approach to biography suggests important criteria for the further study of the 16th-century mind. In his approach to historical characters Erasmus followed no rigid pattern. He was at his brilliant best when crystallizing the course of a life in some major events. To the thorough examination of such chosen aspects he could apply the full vigour of his critical intelligence. In the process, his excellent memory for *topoi* gleaned from Aristotle, Cicero, and Quintilian as well as from Plutarch and Suetonius cooperated with his own powerful observation. That commonplace and personal observation entered each portrait in original synthesis is cogent proof of Erasmus' sense of individuality.

However, it might be argued that it was precisely Erasmus' highly developed sense of individuality which did not permit him to tackle biography more often as his perception of the enigma of personality was all too accurate and the widespread incomprehension of his own individual ways all too painful. When he did write biography the skilful description of individual characteristics may well be his greatest merit, but it was not his ultimate concern. Not the individual as such deserved the fullest attention, but the individual act of participation in the consensus of *philosophia Christi*.

He believed that individual freedom of action was subordinate to compliance with the precepts of true Christianity, a compliance that was possible before and after Christ's incarnation. In the same way he thought the flux of human history and the fluctuations in the course of the individual human life were subordinate to a static and lasting quality. As he did with history as a whole, he viewed the individual *sub specie aeternitatis*. The individual, he thought, was centered upon an inner focal point, but the central point itself was a mirror, clear or cloudy, as may be the case, for the universal individuality of Christ.

CONCLUSION

Erasmus' doubts about the value of most historical writing were at first, it seems, a lonely cry in the wilderness. His own views on history and even his concept of individuality evoked little immediate response. Today, their full significance emerges from our knowledge of the subsequent currents ranging from the historical Pyrrhonism of the early Enlightenment [1] to the historicism of the Ranke school. Erasmus' work appealed to the Age of Reason; despite his general popularity, however, there is no evidence that the enlightened fathers of modern historical thought copied from the very pages examined in this study. Erasmus was no innovator. His influence upon later generations cannot be likened to grafting neatly labelled scions upon new branches; but it may be seen as a process of osmosis, visible only if the entire frame of mind is considered. In this sense, the findings of the preceding pages may be recalled as we glean some comparable features of the later epoch from F. Meinecke's *Die Entstehung des Historismus.*

One cannot entirely disregard Erasmus when considering the place of the 3rd Earl of Shaftesbury in the development of historical thought. The author of *An Essay on the Freedom of Wit and Humour, A Letter concerning Enthusiasm,* and *An Inquiry concerning Virtue or Merit* was indebted to the English humanist ideals of lay piety, Platonizing, and aristocratic liberty. Meinecke speaks of Shaftesbury's freely joyful and pious worldliness ("*freie Weltfreudigkeit und Weltfrömmigkeit*") which tended to correlate high intellectual culture with political freedom. Shaftesbury's profound moralism disparaged priestly government, both Roman and Anglican, in favour of an "inward way of contemplation and divine love". The stress he laid on "the inward form and structure" or the "inward character" of personality amount to an enthusiastic assertion of individuality. [2]

More immediate was Erasmus' influence upon a line of historical thought that Meinecke traces from Sebastian Franck to Gottfried Arnold and Voltaire. [3] Its main achievement was the determined selection of the valuable aspects of the past from among the mass of insignificant ones. Like Erasmus

---

[1] Cf. P. Hazard, *La crise de la conscience européenne,* Paris 1935, 1.45ff.
[2] F. Meinecke, *Die Entstehung des Historismus* (Werke, vol. 3), Munich 1959, 16-27; cf. 202ff. on Hume's *Essay of Superstition and Enthusiasm* and 274ff. on the progress of *Weltfrömmigkeit* to Burke, Herder, Gœthe, and Ranke.
[3] Ibid. 83f.

and Franck before him, Arnold celebrated against the background of a hostile "world" the few truly pious individuals before and after Christ. In statically conceived "inspired souls" he invariably found the touchstones for his judgment of universal history: "one and the same kind of comedy and tragedy is continously acted in the world, only that at any moment different persons participate". [4]

In a different, totally secularized way that replaced the criterion of faith by that of reason, Voltaire too engaged in gathering a little precious ore from history's vast screes. He refreshed his eye at the sight of a few fertile valleys amid a historical desert of rocks and precipices. [5] Where Erasmus had turned away in resignation, feeling that historians normally deal with the wrong things, Voltaire confidently replaced traditional concepts with his own interpretation of universal history based on a new ideal of universal civilization. Erasmus' work implies awareness of the distinctive physiognomy and the peculiar ring in the voice of chosen historical epochs, but he could not present them in historical pictures as did Voltaire. The latter, in fact, developed his understanding of *zeitgeist* from the same basis of unheroic pacifism and with the same disregard of political personalities and concepts that had characterized Erasmus. [6]

Even though insisting that the past could and should be interpreted, Erasmus denounced the most widely accepted interpretations and thus helped to pave the way for the historical Pyrrhonism of the Enlightenment. As Meinecke shows, a similar transitional stage is represented later in the work of Goethe. While approaching a profound and constructive understanding of history which was to make an impact both on Ranke and Burckhardt, Goethe set forth enough criticism of history to give his statements the same oscillating and equivocal character we noticed in Erasmus' work. Goethe once remarked that "... it has a decidedly comical bent to consider how one wants to know with assurance about things long past". Many of his critical comments on history contain a similar dose of piercing commonsense. [7]

As a self-conscious genius, Goethe fully realized that of all things past the individual was the most unknowable. His dictum *"Individuum est ineffabile"* has appropriately been chosen as a central pillar in constructing a mental bridge from Goethe's individualism to Burckhardt's concept of the emerging sense of individuality in the Renaissance. [8] This construction might well be extended further back to Voltaire and Erasmus. For Goethe, as for Erasmus, the inexpressible quality of the individual did not constitute an impasse: in the total mass of individual opinions subject to human error

---

[4] Ibid. 45-53; cf. E. Seeberg, *Gottfried Arnold*, Meerane 1923, 280ff.

[5] F. Meinecke 73ff, esp. 115; cf. W. Kaegi, *Historische Meditationen,* vol. 1 (Zurich 1942), 223ff.: Voltaire und der Zerfall des christlichen Geschichtsbildes. For Voltaire's and Goethe's views of Erasmus: W. Kaegi, Erasmus im achtzehnten Jahrhundert, *Gedenkschrift,* Basel 1936, 205-227.

[6] F. Meinecke esp. 103, 111.

[7] Ibid. 507.

[8] W. Kaegi, *Jacob Burckhardt* 3.719ff; F. Meinecke 468.

there lay a hidden sediment of truth that was no longer liable to rational doubt and proof. This was the "consensus" to which Erasmus appealed in the controversy over Free Will. Goethe, in turn, would say that "only mankind in its entirety is the true man". [9] The same concept of universal individuality which Erasmus had respected in Christ, the "prototype", Goethe found established by the secret agencies of nature that tied the individuals to their biological prototypes. [10] Returning to the historical cosmos, Goethe once spoke of "the one gratifying thing about history, that the real men of all times pre-announce one another, anticipate each other, and pave the way for each other". In a more positive vein he spoke of the "hymn of mankind, listened to with pleasure even by the deity" which was audible to him through all epochs and regions, at time in solo parts and then again in full chorus. [11]

Goethe sensed a dramatic quality of history which is equally bound to recall Erasmus. Voltaire's literary work showed a progression from the theatre to history; Goethe intuitively preferred dramatic form to express his historical visions. The 16th century, in particular, offered to him an overpowering and confusing sight that could best be expressed as a gigantic play on the stage; [12] hence his life-long wrestling with the material of Faust. As was the case with Erasmus, Goethe chose the *theatrum historiae* to reveal the unseverable ties between the spheres of the particular and the general, the individual and the universal, the transient and the eternal. Suffice it to remember the final chorus of the *Faust* drama:

> *Alles Vergängliche*
> *ist nur ein Gleichnis;*
> *das Unzulängliche,*
> *hier wirds Ereignis...*

---

[9] Ibid. 527; J.W. Gœthe, *Dichtung und Wahrheit* 9 (*Gedenkausgabe,* ed. E. Beutler, Zurich 1948, 10.425): "... dann tritt das schöne Gefühl ein, dass die Menschheit zusammen erst der wahre Mensch ist, und der einzelne nur froh und glücklich sein kann, wenn er den Mut hat, sich im Ganzen zu fühlen."

[10] F. Meinecke 537f.: "Man könnte seine ganze Geschichtsauffassung einen universellen Individualismus nennen, wobei man nur im Auge behalten muss, dass zwischen dem Universellen und dem jeweilig Individuellen die ganze Kette von Ur- und Naturformen menschlichen Lebens und Wirkens ... mitempfunden und oft auch ausgedrückt wurde."

[11] Ibid. 538; J.W. Gœthe, *Schriften zur Farbenlehre* (Beutler 16.340, 420): "Betrachtet man die einzelne frühere Ausbildung der Zeiten, Gegenden, Ortschaften, so kommen uns aus der dunklen Vergangenheit überall tüchtige und vortreffliche Menschen ... entgegen. Der Lobgesang der Menschheit, dem die Gottheit so gerne zuhören mag, ist niemals verstummt, und wir selbst fühlen ein göttliches Glück, wenn wir die durch alle Zeiten und Gegenden verteilten harmonischen Ausströmungen, bald in einzelnen Stimmen, in einzelnen Chören, bald fugenweise, bald in einem herrlichen Vollgesang vernehmen."

[12] F. Meinecke 459f., 507f.: "Die Weltgeschichte wurde ihm nicht, wie später für Ranke, zu einem individuellen Gesamtphänomen. ... Geschichte war ihm letzten Endes der Teil eines ewigen Schauspiels, in dem der zeitliche Ablauf Mittel zum Zweck einer ewig neugebärenden Schöpfung wird."

Overcome by similar feelings, Goethe's Wilhelm Meister exclaims, when introduced to the "Hall of the Past": "with equal propriety one might name it the Hall of the Present, or of the Future. For so everything has been, and so everything will be. Nothing is transitory, save the mortal who beholds and enjoys it all". [13]

The circles of the Enlightenment and of Romanticism could no doubt afford many more parallels to Erasmus' view of history. They might also expose significant differences. Erasmus' small confidence in the notion of development alone will clearly remove him from the immediate beginnings of historicism. However, it was not the task of this study to trace the ancestry of historicism, nor indeed to write the history of Erasmianism. The purpose of our investigation seems well accomplished if the few parallels here outlined have helped to give evidence of the validity of Erasmus' grappling with the problems of history.

---

[13] J.W. Gœthe, *Wilhelm Meisters Lehrjahre* 8.5 (Beutler 7.580).

APPENDIX

(The following preface, repeatedly referred to in this study, is here quoted in full since it was not included in the Leyden edition of Erasmus' works. Nor was it reprinted in Allen's edition of Erasmus' correspondence.)

Secundus tomus Operum D. Aurelii Augustini ... complectens illius Epistolas ... emendatus per Des. Erasmum Roterodamum, Froben, Basel 1528 [published in 1529], verso of titlepage:
DES. ERASMUS ROTERODAMUS PIO LECTORI S. D.

Ex calce secundi libri *Retractationum,* item ex epistola quae praefixa est *Catalogo haereseon ad Quodvultdeum,* satis quidem perspicuum est id temporis nec epistolas nec populares orationes ab Augustino fuisse diges-
5 tas. Nec post id ab eo curatum vel illud arguit, quod in hoc volumine neque temporum neque personarum neque materiarum ulla videtur habita ratio. Certius autem id arguit, quod quaedam admixtae fuerant quae primo statim gustu deprehendebantur Augustini non esse, quas addita censura notavimus: nonnullae simpliciter confictae, quod genus sunt illae Bonifacii ad Augustinum, Augustini ad Bonifacium. Nullam tamen omnino loco
10 movimus praeter unam et vehementer prolixam et insigniter illitteratam, ne id quidem facturi, nisi eadem in tomis [sequentibus] haberetur. Tanta nobis cautio fuit, ne quis quid de nostra queri possit industria. Ad haec inspersae sunt nonnullae quas Augustinus ipse in *Retractationibus* libros appellat. Quanquam interdum subdifficile est epistolam a libro distinguere, Augusti-
15 nus alicubi sic loquitur, quasi brevitas aut prolixitas tribuat adimatve nomen epistolae verius quam orationis genus aut argumenti ratio, prae-sertim quum hoc exemplum ab Apostolis venerit, ut argumenta quamvis seria committerentur epistolis. Siquidem exceptis *Evangeliis,* quo nomine complectimur et *Apostolorum gesta,* praeter epistolas nihil scripto prodi-
20 derunt, sed ea de rebus haud quaquam familiaribus tum quas vellent ab omnibus legi. Alicubi putat epistolam non videri, quae non praeferat nomen et scribentis et eius ad quem scribitur. Et sane sunt aliquot quas vere possis epistolas dicere, referentes familiare quiddam et instar humani colloquii, licet perpaucae.

25 Verum hac de re libero esto suum cuique iudicium. Illud ausim affir-mare non alio in opere magis elucere sanctissimi viri pietatem, charitatem, mansuetudinem, humanitatem, civilitatem, studium crediti gregis, amorem concordiae et zelum domus Dei. Ut satagit, ut molitur, ut se vertit in omnia [cf. 1. *Corinthians* 9.22] quoties affulsit aliqua spes pertrahendi vel
30 paganum ad Christum vel haereticum ad Ecclesiae communionem. Ut se

submittit, ut, iuxta Paulum [*Galatians* 4.20], mutat vocem suam, undi-
quaque venans occasionem excitandae propagandaeque pietatis, ubicunque
sentit aliquam bonae mentis scintillam residere. Cui mulierculae, cui ple-
beio, cui aulico, cui pagano, cui haeretico non prompte, mansuete blandeque
35 respondet? Quam anxia sollicitudine pro sceleratissimis nec una morte
dignis Circumcellionibus intercedit ! Quis maiori studio pro suis amicis
interpellavit quam ille pro suis hostibus? Quanto nixu parturit omnes
Christo, quam gratulatur resipiscentibus, quam sollicite prospicit pericli-
tantibus, quam sedulo docet errantes, mederi studens omnibus, perdere
40 neminem. Quam misere uritur ad quodvis exortum offendiculum! Videas
vere gallinam Evangelicam [*Matthew* 23.37], sollicitam et anxiam ut sub
alas colligat foveatque pullos suos. In nonullis epistolis agnoscere licebit
et illud forense dicendi genus quod Graeci δικανικόν appellant, praecipue
quum agit adversus Donati factionem, nec deest argumentorum subtilitati,
45 quae illi peculiaris est δείνωσις. Verum sive docet, sive corripit, sive
pugnat cum deploratis hostibus, nusquam tamen non sentias Christianae
charitatis nativam dulcedinem ut, si tamen congruit haec collatio, mihi
videatur quendam e comoedia referre Mitionem [Micio: cf. Terence,
Adelphi], qui tum etiam mitis est quum obiurgat maxime. In hoc uno, velut
50 in speculo, contemplari licet episcopum qualem depinxit Paulus [1. *Timo-
thy* 3.2-4] : ἀνεπίληπτον, νηφάλιον, σώφρονα, κόσμιον, φιλόξενον, διδακτικὸν,
μὴ πάροινον, μὴ πλήκτην, μὴ αἰσχροκερδῆ, ἀλλ᾽ ἐπιεικῆ, ἄμαχον, ἀφιλάργυ-
ρον, [*Titus* 1.7-9] μὴ αὐθάδη, μὴ ὀργίλον, φιλάγαθον, ἐγκρατῆ, ὅσιον,
δίκαιον. ἀντεχόμενον τοῦ κατὰ τὴν διδαχὴν πιστοῦ λόγου, δυνατὸν καὶ παρα-
55 καλεῖν ἐν τῇ διδασκαλίᾳ τῇ ὑγιαινούσῃ καὶ τοὺς ἀντιλέγοντας ἐλέγχειν μετὰ
πάσης πραότητος. Ad hoc speculum si sese contemplentur episcopi et qui
episcoporum functionem occupant theologi, pudebit, opinor, quosdam sui
supercilii cum inscitia coniuncti, pudebit saevitiae cum impuris moribus
60 copulatae.

Ex aliis Augustini libris perspicere licebit qualis fuerit adhuc infans
in Christo, ex aliis qualis fuerit iuvenis, ex aliis qualis senex ; ex hoc uno
volumine semel totum Augustinum cognosces. Uberiores fructus nobis
dedisset illud ingenium, si in Italia Galliave vel nasci vel vivere contigisset.
65 Rudis erat Africa, voluptatum avida, studiorum inimica, curiosarum rerum
appetens. Unde frequenter exercent illum quaestionibus subfrivolis nec
multum facientibus ad pietatem, et ad suae gentis affectus saepe cogitur
attemperare calamum. Verum tali excolendo senticeto tali opus erat agricola. Quanquam digniora lectu scripturus erat, si vel ad Romanorum aut
70 Graecorum iudicia se composuisset vel minus indulsisset simplicium imperi-
tiae. Sed Christiana charitas prius habet prodesse quamplurimis quam
probari praecipuis, fraternae salutis quam suae gloriae sitientior. Quosdam
autem, praecipue mulierculas, pia quaedam habebat ambitio, pulchrum
esse ducentes qualecunque scriptum impetrasse ab episcopo. Ita factum
75 est ut, dum vir pius omnium votis obsequitur, minus alicubi satisfaciat
lectori fastidioso. Vix quenquam crediturum opinor, quantum mihi sudoris
exhaustum sit in tollendis mendis ac reponenda sermonis confusissima
distinctione. Sed ea demum perfecta est eleemosyna quae confertur
nescienti — generosior etiam quae confertur aversanti. Haec Christo foene-
80 ramus, non hominibus, quorum vix credibilem ingratitudinem in nimium
multis experimur. Quanquam horum malitia nequaquam nos a benefaciendi
studio deterrebit unquam: cum optimae fidei debitore nobis res est.

104

Ne quid omittam, ab huius voluminis calce resecuimus loquacissimam coronidem sub titulis Cyrilli, subito Latine loquentis et Augustini Graeco
85 male [rather: peius] Latine scribentis, impudentissime confictam. Cuius tamen legendae si quem forte tenet libido, reperiet inter ea quae divi Hieronymi tomis adiuncta sunt. Illic expleat sese affatim, qui talibus capitur deliciis. Haec, cordate lector, fac evoluas attente, non poenitebit insumpti temporis. Bene vale.

90   Datum Basileae an. 1527 mense octobri.

———————

INDEX

ACHEVÉ D'IMPRIMER
AUX « PRESSES DE SAVOIE », AMBILLY-ANNEMASSE (H-S.),
EN DÉCEMBRE 1966